# Frame Semantics in NLP 2014

AA004618

# A Workshop in Honor of Chuck Fillmore (1929-2014)

**Held at ACL 2014**

## Baltimore, Maryland, USA
## 27 June 2014

**ISBN: 978-1-63439-210-5**

**Printed from e-media with permission by:**

Curran Associates, Inc.
57 Morehouse Lane
Red Hook, NY 12571

**Some format issues inherent in the e-media version may also appear in this print version.**

Copyright© (2014) by the Association for Computational Linguistics
All rights reserved.

Printed by Curran Associates, Inc. (2014)

For permission requests, please contact the Association for Computational Linguistics
at the address below.

Association for Computational Linguistics
209 N. Eighth Street
Stroudsburg, Pennsylvania 18360

Phone: 1-570-476-8006
Fax: 1-570-476-0860

acl@aclweb.org

**Additional copies of this publication are available from:**

Curran Associates, Inc.
57 Morehouse Lane
Red Hook, NY 12571 USA
Phone: 845-758-0400
Fax: 845-758-2634
Email: curran@proceedings.com
Web: www.proceedings.com

# Introduction

Chuck Fillmore received the Association for Computational Linguistics' Lifetime Achievement Award in July 2012. We see this workshop, held in conjunction with the annual ACL meeting, barely four months since Chuck's passing on February 13, 2014, as an especially fitting occasion to honor Chuck and his contributions to the field.

Those who have had the privilege of knowing Chuck also know that his kindness, humanity, and generosity cannot be surpassed. Those who have had the good fortune of studying with Chuck have learned that his guidance and wisdom, in matters of life at least as much as in those of language, will remain forever. Those who have had the even better fortune of working closely with Chuck in particular throughout the development of FrameNet also have had the great pleasure of witnessing the sheer delight that he brought to his work, and that he shared with his students, colleagues, and friends.

Chuck's career extended for over fifty years, during which time he was professor of linguistics at the Ohio State University and the University of California, Berkeley. Chuck arrived in Berkeley after ten years at OSU, which included a year at the Center for Advanced Studies in the Behavioral Sciences at Stanford University. Chuck's legendary humility belied his keen intellect and profound insight about the nature of language and how we, linguists and computational linguists, ought to think about language, also for machine processing, an effort in which he began to engage during his early days at Ohio State. Chuck's equally legendary wit served as a brilliant pedagogical technique and an endearing personality trait.

Any attempt to summarize Chuck's research in a limited space would necessarily fail. Nevertheless, we would be remiss were we not to invoke Chuck's contributions to the subfields of syntax, semantics, pragmatics, lexicon, and grammar. A number of relatively early papers came to be very important works and remain so to this day, not simply for historical purposes. An early contribution to transformational grammar that introduced cyclic rules applying to small units of structure rings of concepts later revived and expanded in Chuck's work with his Berkeley colleagues in developing Construction Grammar. "The Case for Case," an often-cited work among linguists of many persuasions, holds the seed of the frame idea that later blossomed into Frame Semantics. The careful reader will identify numerous FrameNet frames in papers about verbs of judging, hitting and breaking, as well as the concept *risk*, the last with lexicographer Sue Atkins, whose influence on Chuck to found FrameNet cannot be underestimated. Chuck's well-known lectures on deixis provided support to the newly emerging field of linguistic pragmatics.

And, of course, the impact of Chuck's research on Natural Language Processing is the subject matter of the invited talks and papers at the workshop whose proceedings we introduce here.

This small collection begins with several contributions that highlight the profound and sometimes under-appreciated role of Chuck's work in computational linguistics. Collin F. Baker ("FrameNet: A Knowledge Base for Natural Language Processing") takes the reader on a journey through time from Chuck's early work on case grammar all the way to FrameNet's current use in natural language processing. Kenneth Church ("The Case for Empiricism (With and Without Statistics)") contextualizes these achievements with respect to the broader developments in the field of computational linguistics. Jerry Hobbs ("Case, Constructions, FrameNet, and the Deep Lexicon") expounds on how Chuck's discoveries contribute to developing what Hobbs calls *deep* theories of lexical meaning, drawing on ideas from psychology and logic.

Two papers relate FrameNet to other resources while presenting ongoing efforts to interlink them. Martha Palmer, Claire Bonial, and Diana McCarthy ("SemLink+: FrameNet, VerbNet and Event Ontologies") discuss FrameNet's relationship to VerbNet and to event ontologies in the SemLink+ project. Nancy Ide

("FrameNet and Linked Data") assesses broader community activities to connect FrameNet with other resources such as WordNet and MASC in the Linguistic Linked Open Data cloud.

Given the subject of the workshop, that a number of contributions focus on practical natural language processing applications is no surprise. Srini Narayanan ("Bridging Text and Knowledge with Frames") presents an overview of sophisticated artificial intelligence and information retrieval applications of FrameNet such as information extraction, question answering, and metaphor detection. Dipanjan Das ("Statistical Models for Frame-Semantic Parsing") describes some of the most advanced algorithms for automatic frame-semantic parsing. Apoorv Agarwal, Daniel Bauer, and Owen Rambow ("Using Frame Semantics in Natural Language Processing") discuss ongoing research projects at Columbia University that exploit FrameNet for producing advanced semantic representations, while highlighting important research challenges for the community.

Finally, two contributions follow Chuck's lead in starting with specific empirical observations about language and then raising broader questions about the nature of semantics. Katrin Erk ("Who Evoked that Frame? Some Thoughts on Context Effects and Event Types") provides an analysis of lexical substitution and examines its bearings on frame semantics. Eduard C. Dragut and Christiane Fellbaum ("The Role of Adverbs in Sentiment Analysis") comment on the role of adverbs in lexical resources for sentiment analysis.

With these papers, we celebrate Chuck's path-breaking contributions to linguistics, and their impact on the allied fields of cognitive psychology, computational linguistics, and artificial intelligence. In so doing, we honor the man whose presence in our midst we will miss far beyond what our meager words can express.

Miriam R. L. Petruck and Gerard de Melo

**Organizers:**

Miriam R. L. Petruck, International Computer Science Institute, Berkeley
Gerard de Melo, Tsinghua University, Beijing

## Table of Contents

# Conference Program

*FrameNet: A Knowledge Base for Natural Language Processing*
Collin Baker

*The Case for Empiricism (With and Without Statistics)*
Kenneth Church

*Case, Constructions, FrameNet, and the Deep Lexicon*
Jerry Hobbs

*SemLink+: FrameNet, VerbNet and Event Ontologies*
Martha Palmer, Claire Bonial and Diana McCarthy

*FrameNet and Linked Data*
Nancy Ide

*Bridging Text and Knowledge with Frames*
Srini Narayanan

*Statistical Models for Frame-Semantic Parsing*
Dipanjan Das

*Using Frame Semantics in Natural Language Processing*
Apoorv Agarwal, Daniel Bauer and Owen Rambow

*Who Evoked that Frame? Some Thoughts on Context Effects and Event Types*
Katrin Erk

*The Role of Adverbs in Sentiment Analysis*
Eduard Dragut and Christiane Fellbaum

# FrameNet: A Knowledge Base for Natural Language Processing

**Collin F. Baker**
International Computer Science Institute
1947 Center St., Suite 600
Berkeley, California 94704 U.S.A.
collinb@icsi.berkeley.edu

## Abstract

Prof. Charles J. Fillmore had a lifelong interest in lexical semantics, and this culminated in the latter part of his life in a major research project, the FrameNet Project at the International Computer Science Institute in Berkeley, California (http://framenet.icsi.berkeley.edu). This paper reports on the background of this ongoing project, its connections to Fillmore's other research interests, and briefly outlines applications and current directions of growth for FrameNet, including FrameNets in languages other than English.

## 1 Introduction

It was my honor to work closely with the late Charles Fillmore as part of the FrameNet project at the International Computer Science Institute in Berkeley, California (http://framenet.icsi.berkeley.edu) from 1997 until this year. It was a blessing to be in contact with that rare combination of a brilliant intellect, a compassionate heart, and genuine humility. This article will discuss where FrameNet fits in the development of Fillmore's major theoretical contributions (case grammar, frame semantics and construction grammar), how FrameNet can be used for NLP, and where the project is headed.

## 2 From Case Grammar to Frame Semantics to FrameNet

The beginnings of case grammar were contemporary with the development of what came to be called the "Standard Theory" of Generative Grammar (Chomsky, 1965), and related "through friendship" to the simultaneous development of Generative Semantics. Fillmore (1968) showed that a limited number of case roles could provide elegant explanations of quite varied linguistic phenomena, such as the differences in morphological case marking between nominative-accusative, nominative-ergative, and active-inactive languages, and anaphoric processes such as subject drop in Japanese. A year later (Fillmore, 1969), after explaining that verbs like *rob* and *steal* require three arguments, the culprit, the loser, and the loot, he continues in the next section to say

> It seems to me, however, that this sort of detail is unnecessary, and that what we need are abstractions from these specific role descriptions, abstractions which will allow us to recognize that certain elementary role notions recur in many situations,... Thus we can identify the culprit of rob and the critic of criticize with the more abstract role of Agent... in general... the roles that [predicates'] arguments play are taken from an inventory of role types fixed by grammatical theory.

But the search for the "correct" minimal set of case roles proved to be difficult and contentious, and it became apparent that some predicators, such as *replace* and *resemble*, required roles which did not fit into the usual categories. In fact, the original case roles (a.k.a. semantic roles, thematic roles, theta roles) were increasingly seen as generalizations over a much larger set of roles which provide more detailed information about the participants in a large variety of situations, described as **semantic frames** (Fillmore, 1976; Fillmore, 1977b).

Thus, the formulation of Frame Semantics should not be seen as a repudiation of the concept of case roles expounded in Fillmore 1968, but rather a recognition of the inadequacy of case roles as a characterization of all the different types of



*Proceedings of Frame Semantics in NLP: A Workshop in Honor of Chuck Fillmore (1929–2014)*, pages 1–5,
Baltimore, Maryland USA, June 27, 2014. ©2014 Association for Computational Linguistics

interactions of participants that can be linguistically significant in using language to describe situations:

> ...[A]s I have conceived them, the repertory of cases is NOT identical to the full set of notions that would be needed to make an analysis of any state or event. ...[A] case frame need not comprise a complete description of all the relevant aspects of a situation, but only a particular piece or section of a situation. (Fillmore (1977a), emphasis in the original)

The concept of frames became part of the academic zeitgeist of the 1960s and 70s. Roger Shank was using the term **script** to talk about situations like eating in a restaurant (Schank and Abelson, 1977) and the term *frame* was being used in a more-or-less similar sense by Marvin Minsky (1974), and Eugene Charniak (1977).

### FrameNet as an Implementation of Frame Semantics

During the late 1980s and early 1990s, much of Fillmore's effort went into joint work with Paul Kay, Catherine O'Connor, and others on the development of Construction Grammar, especially on linking constructions in which the semantic attributes of various constituents were represented by thematic roles such as Agent, Patient, Experiencer, Stimulus, etc., (cf. Levin (1993)). But semantic frames were always presupposed in Fillmore's discussion of Construction Grammar (e.g. Kay and Fillmore (1999)), just as Construction Grammar was always presupposed in discussions of Frame Semantics. In fact, some of the incidental references to semantic frames in the literature on construction grammar imply the existence of very sophisticated frame semantics. At the same time, Fillmore was becoming involved with the lexicographer Sue Atkins, and increasingly thinking about what the dictionary would look like, if freed from the limitations of publishing on paper (Fillmore and Atkins, 1994) and based on corpus data.

The FrameNet Project (Fillmore and Baker, 2010; Ruppenhofer et al., 2010a) at the International Computer Science Institute was launched in 1997, as an effort to produce a lexicon of English that is both human- and machine-readable, based on the theory of Frame Semantics and supported by annotating corpus examples of the lexical items. In part, FrameNet (FN) can be thought of as the implementation of a theory that was already well-developed, but, like other annotation projects, we have found that the process of annotating actual text has also pushed the development of the theory.

So what is a frame? Ruppenhofer et al. (2006) define a frame as "a script-like conceptual structure that describes a particular type of situation, object, or event along with its participants and props." Frames are generalizations over groups of words which describe similar states of affairs and which could be expected to share similar sets of roles, and (to some extent) similar syntactic patterns for them. In the terminology of Frame Semantics, the roles are called frame elements (FEs), and the words which evoke the frame are referred to as lexical units (LUs). A lexical unit is thus a Saussurian "sign", an association between a form and a meaning; the form is a lemma with a given part of speech, the meaning is represented as a semantic frame plus a short dictionary-style definition, which is intended to differentiate this lexical unit from others in the same frame. Each lexical unit is equivalent to a word sense; if a lemma has more than one sense, it will be linked to more than one LU in more than one frame; e.g. the lemma *run*.v (and all its word forms, *run, ran*, and *running*) is linked to several frames (**Self-motion, Operating a system**, etc.).

Some of this literature refers to two types of entities, **frames** and **scenes** (Fillmore, 1977c). However, early in the process of defining the FN data structure, it was recognized that more than two levels of generality might be needed, so it was decided to create only one type of data object, called a frame, and to define relations between frames at various levels of generality. Therefore, the term scene is not used in FrameNet today, although some frames which define complex events have the term **scenario** as part of their names, such as the **Employer's scenario**, with subframes **Hiring, Employing** and **Firing**.

In many cases, the framal distinctions proposed by Fillmore in early work are directly reflected in current FN frames, as in the pair of frames **Stinginess** and **Thriftiness**, discussed in Fillmore (1985). In other cases, the frame divisions in FN differ from those originally proposed, as in the division of the original Commerce frame into three frames, **Commerce, Commerce_buy** and **Commerce_sell**, which are connected by frame-to-frame relations.

Because Frame Semantics began in the study of verbs and valences, there was emphasis initially on representing events, but the principle that a conceptual gestalt can be evoked by any member of a set of words also applies to relations, states, and entities, and the evoking words can be nouns, adjectives, adverbs, etc., as well as verbs. For example, the **Leadership** frame contains both nouns (*leader, headmaster*, *maharaja*), and verbs (*lead*, *command*); FEs in the **Leadership** frame include the LEADER and the GOVERNED, as in [$_{\text{LEADER}}$ Kurt Helborg] is the CAPTAIN [$_{\text{GOVERNED}}$ of the Reiksguard Knights].

## 3 Applications of FrameNet

Underlying other applications is the need for middle-ware to carry out automatic semantic role labeling (ASRL). Beginning with the work of Gildea and Jurafsky (2000; 2002), many researchers have built ASRL systems trained on the FrameNet data (Erk and Padó, 2006; Johansson and Nugues, 2007; Das et al., 2013), some of which are freely available. Other groups have built software to suggest new LUs for existing frames, or even new frames (Green, 2004)

Typical end-user applications for FrameNet include Question answering (Sinha, 2008) and information extraction (Mohit and Narayanan, 2003), and using FrameNet data has enabled some improvements on systems attempting the RTE task (Burchardt, 2008). The FrameNet website lists the intended uses for hundreds of users of the FrameNet data, including sentiment analysis, building dialog systems, improving machine translation, teaching English as a second language, etc. The FrameNet team have an active partnership with Decisive Analytics Corporation, which is using FN-based ASRL as for event recognition and tracking for their govenment and commercial clients.

## 4 Some Limitations and Extensions of the FrameNet Model

FrameNet works almost entirely on edited text, so directly applying the ASRL systems trained on current FN data will probably give poor results on, e.g. Twitter feeds or transcribed conversation. FrameNet also works strictly within the sentence, so there is no direct way to deal with text coherence, although FrameNet annotation does indicate when certain core FEs are missing from a sentence, which typically indicates that that they are realized elsewhere in the text. This feature can be used to link arguments across sentences (Ruppenhofer et al., 2010b).

**Technical terms and Proper Nouns:**

FrameNet has taken as its mandate to cover the "core" lexicon of English, words in common use, whose definitions are established by their usage. The number of senses per word is known to increase with the frequency of occurrence Zipf (19491965), so the most frequent words are likely to be the most polysemous and therefore both the most important and the most challenging for NLP. In general, the FrameNet team have assumed that technical vocabulary, whose definitions are established by domain experts, will be handled in terminologies for each domain, such as the Medical Subject Headings of the U.S. National Library of Medicine (`https://www.nlm.nih.gov/mesh/meshhome.html`) and the Department of Defense Dictionary of Military Terms (`http://www.dtic.mil/doctrine/dod_dictionary/`). For similar reasons, FrameNet does not annotate proper nouns, also known in NLP as named entities. FrameNet cannot and has no reason to compete with the on-line resources for these domains, such as Wikipedia, lists of male and female personal names, and gazetteers. On the other hand, Frame Semantic resources have been produced in several specialized domains: Thomas Schmidt created a Frame-Semantic analysis of the language associated with soccer (in German, English, and French) (Schmidt, 2008), `http://www.kictionary.com`; and lexica in the legal domain have been produced for Italian (Venturi et al., 2009) and Brazilian Portuguese (Bertoldi and Oliveira Chishman, 2012).

**Negation and Conditionals:**

FrameNet does not have representations for negation and conditional sentences. The words *never*.adv and *seldom*.adv are LUs in the **Frequency** frame, but there is no recognition of their status as negatives. The general approach which the FrameNet team has proposed would be to treat negative expressions as parts of constructs licensed by constructions which have a "negation" frame as their meaning pole, and license negative polarity items over some scope in the sentence, but defining that scope is a notoriously difficult problem. We are just beginning to work a mental spaces approach to the related problem of conditional sentences, cf. Dancygier and Sweetser (2005) and Sweetser (2006). FrameNet does not include the word *if*, but does include both LUs and annotation for a number of modal verbs and other types of nouns and adjectives which can be used to express conditionality, incuding the following:

| **Frame** | : **LUs** |
|---|---|
| **Possibility** | : *can, could, might, may* |
| **Capability** | : *able*.a, *ability*.n, *can*.v, *potential*.n/a, ... |
| **Likelihood** | : *likely*.a, *might*.v, *may*.v, *must*.v, *possible*.a, ... |

## 5 Future directions: Expert curation vs. rapid growth

After almost two decades of work at varying levels of intensity, depending on funding, FrameNet contains almost 1200 Semantic Frames, covering almost 13,000 word senses (Lexical Units) , documented with almost 200,000 manual annotations. This is bigger than a toy lexicon, but far fewer LUs than WordNet or other lexicons derived automatically from the web. By virtue of expert curation, the FrameNet lexical database contains a wealth of semantic knowledge that is unique. The database is freely available from the FrameNet website.

One challenge we face now is finding a way to greatly expand FrameNet in a more cost-effective way while preserving the accuracy and richness of the annotation. We have recently done some small-scale experiments on crowd-sourcing various parts of the process in partnership with colleagues at Google, and the preliminary results are encouraging.

Another challenge comes as a result of the success of Frame Semantics as an interlingua (Boas, 2009). There are now projects building FrameNet-style lexical databases for many different languages; funded projects are creating FrameNets for German, Spanish, Japanese, Swedish, Chinese, French and Arabic; smaller efforts have created Frame Semantics-based resources for many other languages, including Italian, Korean, Polish, Bulgarian, Russian, Slovenian, Hebrew, and Hindi. Some are produced almost entirely via manual annotation, while others are being created semi-automatically. The good news is that the general result seems to be that the frames devised for English can be used for the majority of LUs in each of these language. The challenge is finding a way to integrate the frame semantic work being done around the world, to create a truly multi-lingual FrameNet.

For more information on all these topics, please visit

`http://framenet.icsi.berkeley.edu`

## References


Anderson Bertoldi and Rove Luiza Oliveira Chishman. 2012. Developing a frame-based lexicon for the Brazilian legal language: The case of the criminal process frame. In Monica Palmirani, Ugo Pagallo, Pompeu Casanovas, and Giovanni Sartor, editors, *AI Approaches to the Complexity of Legal Systems*, volume 7639 of *Lecture Notes in Computer Science*, pages 256–270. Springer Berlin Heidelberg.

Hans C. Boas, editor. 2009. *Multilingual FrameNets in Computational Lexicography: Methods and Applications*. Mouton de Gruyter.

Aljoscha Burchardt. 2008. *Modeling Textual Entailment with Role-Semantic Information*. Ph.D. thesis, Universität des Saarlandes.

Eugene Charniak. 1977. Framed PAINTING: The representation of a common sense knowledge fragment. *Cognitive Science*, 1(4):235–264.

Noam Chomsky. 1965. *Aspects of the Theory of Syntax*. MIT Press, Cambridge, MA.

Barbara Dancygier and Eve Sweetser. 2005. *Mental spaces in grammar: conditional constructions*. Cambridge University Press, Cambridge, UK; New York.

Dipanjan Das, Desai Chen, André F. T. Martins, Nathan Schneider, and Noah A. Smith. 2013. Frame-Semantic parsing. *Computational Linguistics*, 40(1).

Katrin Erk and Sebastian Padó. 2006. Shalmaneser – a flexible toolbox for semantic role assignment. In *Proceedings of the fifth International Conference on Language Resources and Evaluation (LREC-2006)*, Genoa, Italy.

Charles J. Fillmore and B.T.S. Atkins. 1994. Starting where the dictionaries stop: The challenge for computational lexicography. In Antonio Zampolli and Sue Atkins, editors, *Computational Approaches to the Lexicon*. Oxford University Press.

Charles J. Fillmore and Collin F. Baker. 2010. A frames approach to semantic analysis. In Bernd Heine and Heiko Narrog, editors, *Oxford Handbook of Linguistic Analysis*, pages 313–341. OUP.

Charles J. Fillmore. 1968. The case for case. In E. Bach and R. Harms, editors, *Universals in Linguistic Theory*. Holt, Rinehart & Winston, New York.

Charles J. Fillmore. 1969. Toward a modern theory of case. In David A Reibel and Sanford A. Shane, editors, *Modern Studies in English: Readings in Transformational Grammar*, pages 361–375. Prentice-Hall, Englewood Cliffs, New Jersey.

Charles J. Fillmore. 1976. Frame semantics and the nature of language. *Annals of the New York Academy of Sciences: Conference on the Origin and Development of Language and Speech*, 280(1):20–32.

Charles J. Fillmore. 1977a. Frame semantics. pages 111–137.

Charles J. Fillmore. 1977b. The need for a frame semantics in linguistics. In Hans Karlgren, editor, *Statistical Methods in Linguistics*. Scriptor.

Charles J. Fillmore. 1977c. Scenes-and-frames semantics. In Antonio Zampolli, editor, *Linguistic Structures Processing*, number 59 in Fundamental Studies in Computer Science. North Holland Publishing.

Charles J. Fillmore. 1985. Frames and the semantics of understanding. *Quaderni di Semantica*, 6(2):222–254.

Daniel Gildea and Daniel Jurafsky. 2000. Automatic labeling of semantic roles. In *ACL 2000: Proceedings of ACL 2000, Hong Kong*.

Daniel Gildea and Daniel Jurafsky. 2002. Automatic labeling of semantic roles. *Computational Linguistics*, 28(3):245–288.

Rebecca Green. 2004. *Inducing Semantic Frames from Lexical Resources*. Ph.D. thesis, University of Maryland, College Park.

Richard Johansson and Pierre Nugues. 2007. LTH: Semantic structure extraction using nonprojective dependency trees. In *Proceedings of the Fourth International Workshop on Semantic Evaluations (SemEval-2007)*, pages 227–230, Prague, Czech Republic, June. Association for Computational Linguistics.

Paul Kay and Charles J. Fillmore. 1999. Grammatical constructions and linguistic generalizations: The what's x doing y? construction. *Language*, 75:1–33.

Beth Levin. 1993. *English Verb Classes and Alternations: A Preliminary Investigation*. University of Chicago Press, Chicago.

Marvin Minsky. 1974. A framework for representing knowledge. Memo 306, MIT-AI Laboratory, June.

Behrang Mohit and Srini Narayanan. 2003. Semantic extraction with wide-coverage lexical resources. In Marti Hearst and Mari Ostendorf, editors, *HLT-NAACL 2003: Short Papers*, pages 64–66, Edmonton, Alberta, Canada, May 27 - June 1. Association for Computational Linguistics.

Josef Ruppenhofer, Michael Ellsworth, Miriam R. L. Petruck, Christopher R. Johnson, and Jan Scheffczyk. 2006. *FrameNet II: Extended Theory and Practice*. International Computer Science Institute, Berkeley, California. Distributed with the FrameNet data.

Josef Ruppenhofer, Michael Ellsworth, Miriam R. L. Petruck, Christopher R. Johnson, and Jan Scheffczyk. 2010a. *FrameNet II: Extended Theory and Practice*. FrameNet Project, September.

Josef Ruppenhofer, Caroline Sporleder, Roser Morante, Collin Baker, and Martha Palmer. 2010b. Semeval-2010 task 10: Linking events and their participants in discourse. In *Proceedings of the Workshop on Semantic Evaluations: Recent Achievements and Future Directions (SEW-2009)*, pages 106–111, Boulder, Colorado, June. Association for Computational Linguistics.

Roger C. Schank and Robert P. Abelson. 1977. *Scripts, Plans, Goals and Understanding: an Inquiry into Human Knowledge Structures*. Lawrence Erlbaum, Hillsdale, NJ.

Thomas Schmidt. 2008. The Kicktionary: Combining corpus linguistics and lexical semantics for a multilingual football dictionary. In Eva Lavric, Gerhard Pisek, Andrew Skinner, and Wolfgang Stadler, editors, *The Linguistics of Football*, number 38 in Language in Performance, pages 11–23. Gunter Narr, Tübingen.

Steve Sinha. 2008. *Answering Questions about Complex Events*. Ph.D. thesis, EECS Department, University of California, Berkeley, Dec.

Eve Sweetser. 2006. Negative spaces: Levels of negation and kinds of spaces. In Stéphanie Bonnefille and Sébastien Salbayre, editors, *Proceedings of the conference "Negation: Form, figure of speech, conceptualization"*, Tours. Groupe de recherches anglo-américaines de l'Université de Tours, Publications universitaires Fran cois Rabelais.

Giulia Venturi, Alessandro Lenci, Simonetta Montemagn, Eva Maria Vecchi, Maria Teresa Sagri, and Daniela Tiscornia. 2009. Towards a FrameNet resource for the legal domain. In *Proceedings of the Third Workshop on Legal Ontologies and Artificial Intelligence Techniques*, Barcelona, Spain, June.

George Kingsley Zipf. 1949[1965]. *Human behavior and the principle of least effort: an introduction to human ecology*. Hafner Pub. Co., New York.

# The Case for Empiricism (With and Without Statistics)

**Kenneth Church**
1101 Kitchawan Road
Yorktown Heights, NY 10589
USA
Kenneth.Ward.Church@gmail.com

## Abstract

These days we tend to use terms like *empirical* and *statistical* as if they are interchangeable, but it wasn't always this way, and probably for good reason. In *A Pendulum Swung Too Far* (Church, 2011), I argued that graduate programs should make room for both Empiricism and Rationalism. We don't know which trends will dominate the field tomorrow, but it is a good bet that it won't be what's hot today. We should prepare the next generation of students for all possible futures, or at least all probable futures. This paper argues for a diverse interpretation of Empiricism, one that makes room for everything from Humanities to Engineering (and then some).

Figure 1: Lily Wong Fillmore (standing) and Charles (Chuck) Fillmore

## 1 Lifetime Achievement Award (LTA)

Since the purpose of this workshop is to celebrate Charles (Chuck) Fillmore, I would like to take this opportunity to summarize some of the points that I made in my introduction to Chuck's LTA talk at ACL-2012.

I had the rather unusual opportunity to see his talk (a few times) before writing my introduction because Chuck video-taped his talk in advance.[1] I knew that he was unable to make the trip, but I had not appreciated just how serious the situation was. I found out well after the fact that the LTA meant a lot to him, so much so that he postponed an operation that he probably shouldn't have postponed (over his doctor's objection), so that he would be able to answer live questions via Skype after the showing of his video tape.

I started my introduction by crediting Lily Wong Fillmore, who understood just how much Chuck wanted to be with us in Korea, but also, just how impossible that was. Let me take this opportunity to thank her once again for her contributions to the video (technical lighting, editing, encouragement and so much more).

For many of us in my generation, C4C, Chuck's "The Case for Case" (Fillmore, 1968) was the introduction to a world beyond Rationalism and Chomsky. This was especially the case for me, since I was studying at MIT, where we learned many things (but not Empiricism).

After watching Chuck's video remarks, I was struck by just how nice he was. He had nice things to say about everyone from Noam Chomsky to Roger Schank. But I was also struck by just how difficult it was for Chuck to explain how important C4C was (or even what it said and why it mattered). To make sure that the international audience wasn't misled by his upbringing and his self-deprecating humor, I showed a page of "Minnesota Nice" stereotypes, while reminding the audience that stereotypes aren't nice, but as stereotypes go, these stereotypes are about as nice as they get.

[1] The video is available online at https://framenet.icsi.berkeley.edu/fndrupal/node/5489.



*Proceedings of Frame Semantics in NLP: A Workshop in Honor of Chuck Fillmore (1929–2014)*, pages 6–9,
Baltimore, Maryland USA, June 27, 2014. ©2014 Association for Computational Linguistics

Chuck, of course, is too nice to mention that Fillmore (1967) had 6000 citations in Google Scholar as of ACL-2012.[2] He also didn't mention that he has another half dozen papers with 1000 or more citations including an ACL paper on FrameNet (Baker *et al*, 1998).[3]

I encouraged the audience to read C4C. Not only is it an example of a great linguistic argument, but it also demonstrates a strong command of the classic literature as well as linguistic facts. Our field is too "silo"-ed. We tend to cite recent papers by our friends, with too little discussion of seminal papers, fields beyond our own, and other types of evidence that go beyond the usual suspects. We could use more "Minnesota Nice."

I then spent a few slides trying to connect the dots between Chuck's work and practical engineering apps, suggesting a connection between morphology and Message Understanding Conference (MUC)-like tasks. We tend to think too much about parsing (question 1), though question 2 is more important for tasks such as information extraction and semantic role labeling.

1. What is the NP (and the VP) under S?
2. Who did what to whom?

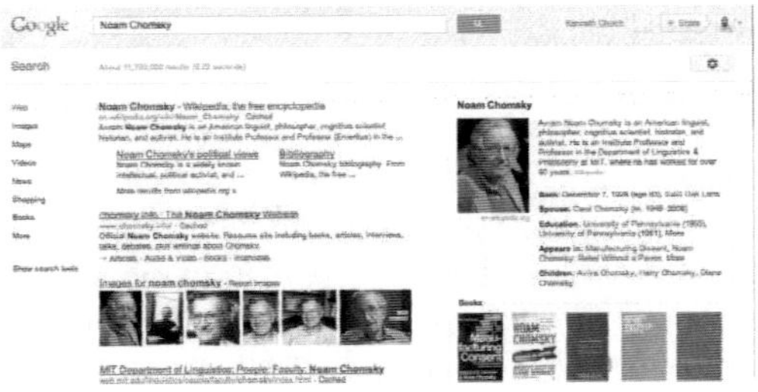

Figure 2: An example of information extraction in commercial practice.

Context-Free Grammars are attractive for languages with more word order and less morphology (such as English), but Case Grammar may be more appropriate for languages with more morphology and less word order (such as Latin, Greek & Japanese). I then gave a short (oversimplified) tutorial on Latin and Japanese grammar, suggesting a connection between Latin cases (e.g., nominative, accusative, ablative, etc.) and Japanese function words (e.g., the subject marker *ga* and the direct object marker *wo*, etc.). From there, I mentioned a few historical connections

- Case Grammar → Frames → FrameNet
- Valency[4] → Scripts (Roger Schank)
- Chuck → Sue Atkins (Lexicography)

The verb "give," for example, requires three arguments: *Jones* (agent) *gave money* (object) *to the school* (beneficiary). In Latin, these arguments are associated with different cases (nominative, accusative, etc.). Under the frame view, similar facts are captured with a *commercial transaction frame*, which connects arguments across verbs such as: *buy, sell, cost* and *spend*.[5]

| VERB | BUYER | GOODS | SELLER | MONEY | PLACE |
|---|---|---|---|---|---|
| *buy* | subject | object | from | for | at |
| *sell* | to | | | | |
| *cost* | indirect object | subject | | object | at |
| *spend* | subject | on | | object | at |

Lexicographers such as Sue Atkins use patterns such as:

- Risk <valued object> for <situation> | <purpose> | <beneficiary> | <motivation>

to address similar alternations. My colleague Patrick Hanks uses a similar pattern to motivate our work on using statistics to find collocations:

- Save <good thing> from <bad situation>

Lexicographers use patterns like this to account for examples such as:

- *Save whales from extinction*
- *Ready to risk everything for what he believes.*

where we can't swap the arguments:

- **Save extinction from whales*

The challenge for the next generation is to move this discussion from lexicography and general linguistics to computational linguistics. Which of these representations are most appropriate for practical NLP apps? Should we focus on part of speech tagging statistics, word order or frames

[2] Citations tend to increase over time, especially for important papers like Fillmore (1967), which has more than 7000 citations as of April 2014.

[3] See framenet.icsi.berkeley.edu for more recent publications such as Ruppenhofer *et al* (2006).

[4] http://en.wikipedia.org/wiki/Valency_(linguistics)

[5] For more discussion of this table, see www.uni-stuttgart.de/ linguistik/ sfb732/ files/ hamm_framesemantics.pdf

(typical predicate-argument relations and collocations)?

Do corpus-based lexicography methods scale up? Are they too manually intensive? If so, could we use machine learning methods to speed up manual methods? Just as statistical parsers learn phrase structure rules such as S → NP VP, we may soon expect machine learning systems to learn valency, collocations and typical predicate-argument relations.

How large do the corpora have to be to learn what? When can we expect to learn frames? In the 1980s, corpora were about 1 million words (Brown Corpus). That was large enough to make a list of common content words, and to train part of speech taggers. A decade later, we had 100 million word corpora such as the British National Corpus. This was large enough to see associations between common predicates and function words such as "save" + "from." Since then, with the web, data has become more and more available. Corpus growth may well be indexed to the price of disks (improving about 1000x per decade). Coming soon, we can expect $1M^2$ word corpora. (Google may already be there.) That should be large enough to see associations of pairs of content words (collocations). At that point, machine learning methods should be able to learn many of the patterns that lexicographers have been talking about such as: *risk valued object for purpose*.

We should train the next generation with the technical engineering skills so they will be able to take advantage of the opportunities, but more importantly, we should encourage the next generation to read the seminal papers in a broad range of disciplines so the next generation will know about lots of interesting linguistic patterns that will, hopefully, show up in the output of their machine learning systems.

## 2 Empirical / Corpus-Based Traditions

As mentioned above, there is a direct connection between Fillmore and Corpus-Based Lexicographers such as Sue Atkins (Fillmore and Atkins, 1992). Corpus-based work has a long tradition in lexicography, linguistics, psychology and computer science, much of which is documented in the Newsletter of the International Computer Archive of Modern English (ICAME).[6] According to Wikipedia,[7] ICAME was co-founded by Nelson Francis, who is perhaps best known for his collaboration with Henry Kučera on the Brown Corpus.[8] The Brown Corpus dates back to the 1960s, though the standard reference was published two decades later (Francis and Kučera, 1982).

The Brown Corpus has been extremely influential across a wide range of fields. According to Google Scholar, the Brown Corpus has more than 3000 citations. Many of these references have been extremely influential themselves in a number of different fields. At least[9] ten of these references have at least 2000 citations in at least five fields:

- Information Retrieval (Baeza-Yates and Ribeiro-Neto, 1999),
- Lexicography (Miller, 1995),
- Sociolinguistics (Biber, 1991),
- Psychology (MacWhinney, 2000)
- Computational Linguistics (Marcus *et al*, 1993; Jurafsky and Martin, 2000; Church and Hanks, 1990; Resnik, 1995)

All of this work is empirical, though much of it is not all that statistical. The Brown Corpus and corpus-based methods have been particularly influential in the Humanities, but less so in other fields such as Machine Learning and Statistics. I remember giving talks at top engineering universities and being surprised, when reporting experiments based on the Brown Corpus, that it was still necessary in the late 1990s to explain what the Brown Corpus was, as well as the research direction that it represented. While many of these top universities were beginning to warm up to statistical methods and machine learning, there has always been less awareness of empiricism and less sympathy for the research direction. These days, I fear that the situation has not improved all that much. In fact, there may be even less room than ever for empirical work (unless it is statistical).

It is ironic how much the field has changed (and how little it has changed). Back in the early 1990s, it was difficult to publish papers that digressed from the strict rationalist tradition that dominated the field at the time. We created the Workshop on Very Large Corpora (WVLC

---

6 http://icame.uib.no/archives/No_1_ICAME_News.pdf

7 http://en.wikipedia.org/wiki/W._Nelson_Francis

8 http://en.wikipedia.org/wiki/Brown_Corpus

9 Google Scholar is an amazing resource, but not perfect. There is at least one error of omission: Manning and Schütze (1999).

evolved into EMNLP) to make room for a little work of a different kind. But over the years, the differences between the main ACL conference and EMNLP have largely disappeared, and the similarities between EMNLP and ICAME have also largely disappeared. While it is nice to see the field come together as it has, it is a shame that these days, it is still difficult to publish a paper that digresses from the strict norms that dominate the field today, just as it used to be difficult years ago to publish papers that digressed from the strict norms that dominated the field at the time. Ironically, the names of our meetings no longer make much sense. There is less discussion than there used to be of the E-word in EMNLP and the C-word in WVLC.

One of the more bitter sweet moments at a WVLC/EMNLP meeting was the invited talk by Kučera and Francis at WVLC-1995,[10] which happened to be held at MIT. Just a few years earlier, it would have been unimaginable that such a talk could have been so appreciated at MIT of all places, given so many years of such hostility to all things empirical.

Their talk was the first and last time that I remember a standing ovation at WVLC/EMNLP, mostly because of their contributions to the field, but also because they both stood up for the hour during their talk, even though they were well past retirement (and standing wasn't easy, especially for Francis).

Unfortunately, while there was widespread appreciation for their accomplishments, it was difficult for them to appreciate what we were doing. I couldn't help but notice that Henry was trying his best to read other papers in the WVLC-1995 program (including one of mine), but they didn't make much sense to him. It was already clear then that the field had taken a hard turn away from the Humanities (and C4C and FrameNet) toward where we are today (more Statistical than Empirical).

## 3 Conclusion

Fads come and fads go, but seminal papers such as "Case for Case" are here to stay. As mentioned above, we should train the next generation with the technical engineering skills to take advantage of the opportunities, but more importantly, we should encourage the next generation to read seminal papers in a broad range of disciplines so they know about lots of interesting linguistic patterns that will, hopefully, show up in the output of their machine learning systems.

[10] http://aclweb.org/anthology//W/W95/W95-0100.pdf

## References


Ricardo Baeza-Yates and Berthier Ribeiro-Neto.1999. *Modern information retrieval*. Vol. 463. ACM Press, New York, NY, USA.

Collin F. Baker, Charles J. Fillmore, and John B. Lowe. 1998. "The berkeley framenet project," *ACL*.

Douglas Biber. 1991. *Variation across speech and writing*. Cambridge University Press.

Kenneth Church. 2011. A pendulum swung too far, *Linguistic Issues in Language Technology*, 6(5).

Kenneth Church and Patrick Hanks. 1990 "Word association norms, mutual information, and lexicography." *Computational linguistics* 16(1): 22-29

Charles J. Fillmore. 1968. "The Case for Case." In Bach and Harms (Ed.): *Universals in Linguistic Theory*. Holt, Rinehart, and Winston, New York, NY, USA, pp. 1-88.

Charles J. Fillmore and Beryl TS Atkins. 1992. "Toward a frame-based lexicon: The semantics of RISK and its neighbors." *Frames, fields, and contrasts*, pp. 75-102, Lawrence Erlbaum Associates, Hillsdale, NJ, USA.

W. Nelson Francis and Henry Kučera. 1982 *Frequency analysis of English usage.* Houghton Mifflin, Boston, MA, USA.

Dan Jurafsky and James H. Martin. 2000 *Speech & Language Processing*. Pearson Education India.

Brian MacWhinney. 2000. *The CHILDES Project: The database*. Vol. 2. Psychology Press.

Christopher D. Manning and Hinrich Schütze. 1999. *Foundations of statistical natural language processing*. MIT Press. Cambridge, MA, USA.

Mitchell P. Marcus, Mary Ann Marcinkiewicz, and Beatrice Santorini. 1993. "Building a large annotated corpus of English: The Penn Treebank." *Computational linguistics* 19(2): 313-330.

George A. Miller. 1995. "WordNet: a lexical database for English." *Communications of the ACM* 38(11): 39-41.

Philip Resnik. 1995. "Using information content to evaluate semantic similarity in a taxonomy." *arXiv preprint cmp-lg/9511007*

Josef Ruppenhofer, Michael Ellsworth, Miriam RL Petruck, Christopher R. Johnson, and Jan Scheffczyk. 2006. *FrameNet II: Extended theory and practice*. framenet.icsi.berkeley.edu

# Case, Constructions, FrameNet, and the Deep Lexicon

**Jerry R. Hobbs**
Information Sciences Institute
University of Southern California
Marina del Rey, California

## Abstract

Three major contributions that Charles Fillmore made in linguistics play an important role in the enterprise of deep lexical semantics, which is the effort to link lexical meaning to underlying abstract core theories. I will discuss how case relates to lexical decompositions, how motivated constructions span the borderline between syntax and semantics, and how the frames of FrameNet provide an excellent first step in deep inference.

## 1 Deep Lexical Semantics

Deep lexical semantics (Hobbs, 2008) is the effort to construct formal theories of abstract phenomena, such as composite entities, the figure-ground relation, scales, change of state, and causality, and to link the most common words in English to these theories with axioms explicating their meanings. This work has been deeply influenced by the work of Charles Fillmore in at least three ways – the insights underlying case grammar, in the importance of being able to represent constructions, and in the development of FrameNet. In this talk I will describe how each of these issues is dealt with in deep lexical semantics. First I will sketch three of the underlying core theories.

Composite Entities and the Figure-Ground Relation: A composite entity is a thing made of other things. This is intended to cover physical objects like a telephone, mixed objects like a book, abstract objects like a theory, and events like a concert. It is characterized by a set of components, a set of properties of the components, a set of relations among its components (the structure), and relations between the entity as a whole and its environment (including its function). The predicate $at$ relates an external entity, the figure, to a component in a composite entity, the ground. Different figures and different grounds give us different meanings for $at$.

Spatial location: Pat is at the back of the store.
Location on a scale: Nuance closed at 58.
Membership in an organization: Pat is now at Google.
Location in a text: The table is at the end of the article.
Time of an event: At that moment, Pat stood up.
Event at event: Let's discuss that at lunch.
At a predication: She was at ease in his company.

When $at$ is specialized in this way, we tap into a whole vocabulary for talking about the domain.

Change of State: The predication $change(e_1, e_2)$ says that state $e_1$ changes into state $e_2$. Its principal properties are that $e_1$ and $e_2$ should have an entity in common – a change of state is a change of state of *something*. States $e_1$ and $e_2$ are not the same unless there is an intermediate state. The predicate $change$ is defeasibly transitive; in fact, backchaining on the transitivity axiom is one way to refine the granularity on processes.

Causality: We distinguish between the "causal complex" for an effect and the concept "cause". A causal complex includes all the states and events that have to happen or hold in order for the effect to occur. We say that flipping a switch causes the light to go on. But many other conditions must be in the causal complex – the light bulb can't be burnt out, the wiring has to be intact, the power has to be on in the city, and so on. The two key properties of a causal complex are that when everything in the causal complex happens or holds, so will the effect, and that everything that is in the



*Proceedings of Frame Semantics in NLP: A Workshop in Honor of Chuck Fillmore (1929–2014)*, pages 10–12,
Baltimore, Maryland USA, June 27, 2014. ©2014 Association for Computational Linguistics

causal complex is relevant in a sense that can be made precise. "Causal complex" is a rigorous or monotonic notion, but its utility in everyday life is limited because we almost never can specify everything in it.

"Cause" by contrast is a defeasible or nonmonotonic notion. It selects out of a causal complex a particular eventuality that in a sense is the "active" part of the causal complex, the thing that isn't necessarily normally true. Flipping the switch, in most contexts, is the action that *causes* the light to come on. Causes are the focus of planning, prediction, explanation, and interpreting discourse, but not diagnosis, since in diagnosis, something that normally happens or holds, doesn't.

As illustrations, here is how two verbs are defined in terms of these core theories. The transitive sense of "move", as in "$x$ moves $y$ from $z$ to $w$" is captured by the axiom

$$\begin{aligned}&move(x, y, z, w)\\ &\quad \equiv cause(x, e_1)\\ &\qquad \wedge change'(e_1, e_2, e_3)\\ &\qquad \wedge at'(e_2, y, z)\\ &\qquad \wedge at'(e_3, y, w)\end{aligned}$$

That is, $x$ causes a change $e_1$ from the state $e_2$ in which $y$ is at $z$ to the state $e_3$ in which $y$ is at $w$. The verb "let" as in "$x$ lets $e$ happen" means $x$ does not cause $e$ not to happen. The axiom is

$$\begin{aligned}&let(x, e)\\ &\quad \equiv not(e_1) \wedge cause'(e_1, x, e_2)\\ &\qquad \wedge not'(e_2, e)\end{aligned}$$

## 2 Case

The various case roles proposed by Filllmore (1968) and many others since then can be understood in terms of the roles entities play in these axiomatic decompositions. In the axiom for $move$, $x$ is the agent. An agent is an entity that is viewed as being capable of initiating a causal chain, and the agent of an action is the agent that initiated it.

What Fillmore originally called the object and has since been called the patient and, more bizarrely, the theme is the entity that undergoes the change of state or location. In the $move$ axiom, $y$ plays this role.

When the property that changes in the object is a real or metaphorical "at" relation, as in $move$, then $Z$ is the source and $w$ is the goal. An instrument is an entity that the agent causes to go through a change of state where this change plays an intermediate role in the causal chain. Other proposed case roles can be analyzed similarly.

The more similar verbs are to "move", the easier it is to assign case labels to their arguments. When verbs are not very similar to "move", e.g., "outnumber", assigning case labels becomes more problematic, a factor no doubt in Fillmore's decision not to utilize a small fixed list in FrameNet.

Nevertheless, the abstractness of the underlying core theories, particularly the theory of composite entities, ensures that this understanding of case applies to the verbal lexicon widely. Thus, although case labels play no formal role in deep lexical semantics, the insights of case grammar can be captured and inform the analyses of specific verb meanings.

## 3 Constructions

In the 1980s Fillmore and his colleagues at Berkeley developed the theory of Construction Grammar (Fillmore et al., 1988). I take constructions to be fragments of language that elemplify general compositional principles, but have a conventionalized meaning which is one of perhaps many meanings licensed by the general lexical and compositional structure, but is the sole, or at least the usual, interpretation normally assigned to it in discourse.

An example will perhaps make this clear. The contraction "let's" has a particular meaning, subsumed by, but much more specific than, "let us". "Let us go." could mean the same as "Let's go," although it sounds stilted. But it could also be something kidnap victims say to the kidnapper. By general principles, "let's go" could have either of these meanings. But in fact it only has the first.

Thus, "let's" can be viewed as a conventionalization of one specific interpretation of "let us". The source interpretation is this: "Let's" is a contraction for "let us". A rule of contraction would tell us that when the string "let us" describes a parameterized situation, the string "let's" can describe the same situation. Thus, the best explanation for the occurrence of "let's" is that it is a contraction of "let us", "Let's" is only used in imperative sentences, so the implicit subject is "you". The verb "to let" means, as in the axiom above, "to not cause not". Thus, "let us go." means "Don't you cause us not to go." So far, this supports both meanings above. Now the set of people designated by "us" may or may not include you in general, but in the desired interpretation it does. One way for *you* to cause *us* not to go, provided you are a part of us, is for you not to go yourself. The sentence "Let's go." tells you not to cause us not to go by not going yourself. This abductive interpretation is straightforwardly represented in a proof graph. This is the conventionalized meaning associated with the "let's" construction.

In normal usage we do not unpack this graph structure, but it nevertheless provides the conventional interpretation's *motivation*, a term I believe I first heard from Fillmore in a discussion group in 1980. The conventional interpretation of "let's go" is not completely arbitrary. We can unpack it, and often need to in interpreting discourse. The reply could be "No, you go alone" or "No, let's stay here." Each of these taps into a different aspect of the conventional interpretation's motivation.

Constructions are not phrases like "let's go" or parameterized phrases like "let's VP" but fragments of a proof graph encoding the motivated syntactic and compositional semantic structure as well as the conventionalized interpretation. They are normally deployed in a block, but they can be effortlessly unpacked when one needs to.

## 4 FrameNet

The FrameNet frames (Baker et al., 2003) can be viewed as providing the first level of axioms mapping words and phrases into underlying core theories. For example, "let" is mapped into a frame of enablement (not-cause-not), along with the verbs "permit" and "allow" and the parameterized phrase "make possible". The frames are not expressed in the FrameNet resource as axioms. However, FrameNet was converted into logical axioms by Ovchinnikova (Ovchinnikova et al. 2013), and she and her colleagues have shown that an abduction engine using a knowledge base derived from these sources is competitive with the best of the statistical systems in recognizing textual entailment and in semantic role labelling.

The FrameNet project, in addition, has demonstrated that a concerted, long-term effort, when intelligently thought out with a sensitivity to the nature of language, can produce a highly valuable resource for deep, knowledge-based processing of natural language. This was certainly among Charles Fillmore's greatest contributions to computational linguistics.

## References

Baker, C., Charles Fillmore, and B. Cronin, 2003. The Structure of the Framenet Database, *International Journal of Lexicography*, Volume 16.3, 281-296.

Fillmore, Charles, 1968, The Case for Case, in Bach and Harms (Eds.), *Universals in Linguistic Theory*, New York: Holt, Rinehart, and Winston, 1-88.

Fillmore, Charles, Paul Kay, and Catherine O'Connor, 1988. Regularity and Idiomaticity in Grammatical Constructions: The Case of *let alone*, *Language*, 64, 501-38.

Hobbs, Jerry R. 2008. Deep Lexical Semantics. *Proceedings of 9th International Conference on Intelligent Text Processing and Computational Linguistics (CICLing-2008)*, Haifa, Israel.

Ovchinnikova, Ekaterina, Niloofar Montazeri, Teodor Alexandrov, Jerry R. Hobbs, Michael C. McCord, and Rutu Mulkar-Mehta. 2013. Abductive Reasoning with a Large Knowledge Base for Discourse Processing. In H. Hunt, J. Bos, and S. Pulman, (Eds.), *Computing Meaning*, 4:104-124.

# SemLink+: FrameNet, VerbNet and Event Ontologies

**Martha Palmer, Claire Bonial**
Department of Linguistics
University of Colorado
Boulder, CO

**Diana McCarthy**
Department of Theoretical and
Applied Linguistics (DTAL)
University of Cambridge

mpalmer/Claire.Bonial@colorado.edu diana@dianamccarthy.co.uk

## Abstract

This paper reviews the significant contributions FrameNet has made to our understanding of lexical resources, semantic roles and event relations.

## 1 Introduction

One of the great challenges of Natural Language Processing (NLP) is the multitude of choices that language gives us for expressing the same thing in different ways. This is obviously true when taking other languages into consideration - the same thought can be expressed in English, French, Chinese or Russian, with widely varying results. However, it is also true when considering a single language such as English. Light verb constructions, nominalizations, idioms, slang, paraphrases, and synonyms all give us myriads of alternatives for "coining a phrase." This causes immense difficulty for NLP systems. No one has made greater contributions to advancing the state of the art of lexical semantics, and its applications to NLP, than Chuck Fillmore. In this paper we focus on the central role that FrameNet has played in our development of SemLink+ and in our current explorations into event ontologies that can play a practical role in accurate automatic event extraction.

## 2 Detecting events

An elusive goal of current NLP systems is the accurate detection of events – recognizing the meaningful relations among the topics, people, places and events buried within text. These relations can be very complex, and are not always explicit, requiring subtle semantic interpretation of the data. For instance, NLP systems must be able to automatically recognize that *Stock prices sank* and *The stock market is falling* can be describing the same event. Such an interpretation relies upon a recognition of the similarity between *sinking* and *falling*, as well as noting the connection between stock *prices* and the stock *market*, and, finally, acknowledgment that they are playing the same role. A key element in event extraction is the identification of the participants of an event, such as the initiator of an action and any parties affected by it. Basically *who* did *what* to *whom, when, where, why* and *how?* Many systems today rely on semantic role labeling to help identify participants, and lexical resources that provide an inventory of possible predicate argument structures for individual lexical items are crucial to the success of semantic role labeling (Palmer,et al., 2010).

## 3 SemLink+ and Semantic Roles

SemLink (Palmer, 2009) is an ongoing effort to map complementary lexical resources: PropBank (Palmer et al., 2005), VerbNet (Kipper et al., 2008), FrameNet (Fillmore et al., 2004), and the recently added OntoNotes (ON) sense groupings (Weischedel, et al., 2011). They all associate semantic information with the propositions in a sentence. Each was created independently with somewhat differing goals, and they vary in the level and nature of semantic detail represented. FrameNet is the



*Proceedings of Frame Semantics in NLP: A Workshop in Honor of Chuck Fillmore (1929–2014)*, pages 13–17,
Baltimore, Maryland USA, June 27, 2014. ©2014 Association for Computational Linguistics

most fine-grained with the richest semantics, VerbNet focuses on syntactically-based generalizations that carry semantic implications, and the relatively coarse-grained PropBank has been shown to provide the most effective training data for supervised Machine Learning techniques. Nonetheless, they can be seen as complementary rather than conflicting, and together comprise a whole that is greater than the sum of its parts. SemLink serves as a platform to unify these resources. The recent addition of ON sense groupings, which can be thought of as a more coarse-grained view of WordNet (Fellbaum, 1998), provides even broader coverage for verbs, and a level of representation that is appropriate for linking between VerbNet class members and FrameNet lexical units, as described below.

SemLink unifies these lexical resources at several different levels. First by providing type-to-type mappings between the lexical units for each framework. For PropBank these are the very coarse-grained rolesets, for VerbNet they are verbs that are members of VerbNet classes, and for FrameNet they are the lexical units associated with each Frame. The same lemma can have multiple PropBank rolesets and can be in several VerbNet classes and FrameNet frames, but always with different meanings. In general, the mappings from PropBank to VerbNet or FrameNet tend to be 1-many, while the mappings between VerbNet and FrameNet are more likely to be 1-1. For example, the verb *hear* has just one coarse-grained sense in PropBank, with the following roleset:

Arg0: hearer
Arg1: utterance, sound
Arg2: speaker, source of sound

This roleset maps to both the *Discover* and *See* classes of VerbNet, and the *Hear* and *Perception_experience* frames of FrameNet.

Then, for each lexical unit, SemLink also supplies a mapping between the semantic roles of PropBank and VerbNet, as well as the roles of VerbNet and FrameNet. PropBank uses very generic labels such as Arg0 and Arg1, which correspond to Dowty's Prototypical Agent and Patient, respectively (Dowty, 1991). PropBank has up to six numbered arguments for core verb specific roles and for adjuncts it has several generally applicable Arg*Modifiers* that have function tag labels such as: M*a*N*ne*R, T*e*MP*oral*, LOC*ation*, DIR*ection*, GO*a*L, etc. VerbNet uses more traditional linguistic thematic role labels, with about 30 in total, and assumes adjuncts (ArgM's) will be supplied by PropBank based semantic role labelers. FrameNet is even more fine-grained and has frame-specific core and peripheral roles called Frame Elements for each frame, amounting to over 2000 individual Frame Element types. For example, *He talked about politics* would receive the following semantic role labels from each framework.[1]

PropBank (talk.01)
$\text{He}_{\text{Arg0}}$ $\text{talked}_{\text{RELATION}}$ about $\text{politics}_{\text{Arg1}}$

VerbNet (Talk-37.5):
$\text{He}_{\text{AGENT}}$ $\text{talked}_{\text{RELATION}}$ about $\text{politics}_{\text{TOPIC}}$

FrameNet (Statement frame):
$\text{He}_{\text{SPEAKER}}$ $\text{talked}_{\text{RELATION}}$ about $\text{politics}_{\text{TOPIC}}$

Thanks to Chuck Fillmore's careful guidance, the rich, meticulously crafted Frames in FrameNet, with their detailed descriptions of all possible arguments and their relations to each other, offer the potential of providing a foundation for inferencing about events and their consequences. In addition FrameNet has from the beginning been inclusive in its addition of nominal and adjectival forms to the Frames, which greatly increases our coverage of all predicating elements (Bonial, et al., 2014). There is also a comprehensive FrameNet Constructicon that painstakingly lists many phrasal constructions, such as "the Xer, the Yer" that cannot be found anywhere else (Fillmore, et al., 2012). Many of these frames, including the constructions, apply equally well to other languages, as evidenced by the various efforts to develop FrameNets in other languages[2] promising a likely benefit to multilingual information

[1] Arg0 maps to Agent maps to Speaker. Arg1 maps to Topic maps to Topic.

[2] See FrameNet projects in other languages listed at https://framenet.icsi.berkeley.edu/fndrupal/framenets_in_other_languages

processing as well. Given the close theoretical ties between PropBank, VerbNet and FrameNet, it should be possible to bootstrap from the successful PropBank-based automatic semantic role labelers to equally accurate FrameNet and VerbNet annotators, and to improve overall semantic role labeling performance (Bauer & Rambow, 2011; Dipanjan, et al., 2010; Giuglea & Moschitti, 2006; Merlo & der Plas, 2009; Yi, et al., 2007). That is one of the primary goals of SemLink.

The first release of SemLink (1.1) contained mappings between these three lexical resources as well as a set of PropBank instances from the Wall Street Journal data with mappings to VerbNet classes and thematic roles (Palmer, 2009). Our most recent release, SemLink 1.2,[3] now includes mappings to FrameNet frames and Frame Elements wherever they are available (FN version 1.5), as well as ON sense groupings (Bonial, et al., 2013). The mapping files between PropBank and VerbNet (version 3.2), and FrameNet have also been checked for consistency and updated to more accurately reflect the current relations between these resources.

This annotated corpus can now be used to train and evaluate VerbNet Class and FrameNet Frame classifiers, to explore clusters of Frame Elements that map to the same VerbNet and PropBank semantic roles, and to evaluate approaches to semantic role labeling that use the type-to-type mappings to bootstrap VerbNet and FrameNet role labels from automatic PropBank semantic role labels.

## 4 Events, Event Types and Subevents

Accurate and informative semantic role labels are an essential component of event extraction, but, although necessary, they are not sufficient. Automatic event detection also requires the ability to distinguish between events which are truly separate, such as *Yesterday, John was throwing a ball to Mary and Bill was flying a kite*, as opposed to related events such as *John was washing the dishes and Mary was drying them.* The second pair could be seen as temporally related subevents of an overall *doing the dishes* or *cleaning up the kitchen* event. It can sometimes be quite challenging to determine the relationship between two events. For instance, earthquakes are quite often associated with the collapse of buildings, as in the following example, *The quake destroyed parts of Sausalito. All tall buildings were demolished.*

Many readers might agree that the *earthquakes* CAUSED the *demolishment of the buildings*. However, are the *building* collapses also SUBEVENTs of the *earthquakes*? Sometimes they happen a few days later, or immediately, simultaneously with the earthquake. Are they both subevents? In general, for accurate event detection, it would be very useful to know which events must precede, must follow, or cannot be simultaneous with, which other events. As discussed in the 2013 NAACL Events workshop and this year's ACL Events workshop, clear, consistent annotation of events and their coreference and causal and temporal relations is a much desired but very challenging goal (Ikuta & Palmer, 2014). Any assistance that can be provided by lexical resources is welcome.

Another very important contribution that FrameNet has made is in the realm of defining these kinds of relations, and others, between frames. Parent-Child Frame to Frame relations can include Inheritance, Subframe, Perspective On, Using, Causative Of, Inchoative of, and there is also a Precedes temporal ordering relation.

The DEFT working group in Richer Event Descriptions has recently been exploring expanding the ACE and ERE event types, and how they can be mapped onto a broader ontological context. Exploring the FrameNet relations that the relevant lexical items participate in has been most informative. We first examined the simple LDC ERE classification of Conflict events, which has *demonstrations* and *attacks* as siblings (ERE guidelines). We find FrameNet's classification of *attacks* as Hostile-Encounters quite useful, and have no argument with it having an Inheritance relation with Intentionally_act, and a Using relation with Taking_sides. *Demonstrations*, on the other hand, come under the Protest Frame, which has a Using relation with Taking_sides. The FrameNet

[3] available for download here: http://verbs.colorado.edu/semlink/

organization of *demonstrations* and *attacks*, although perfectly justifiable, doesn't map neatly onto the LDC organization since, although they are close, they are not siblings. However, by also considering SUMO (Niles & Pease, 2001), the Predicate Matrix (de Lacalle , et al., 2014), WordNet and VerbNet, we were able to develop the upper level partial Event Ontology given in Figure 1, which comfortably incorporates the ERE and FrameNet relations within a broader framework, preserving the key aspects of each.

We are now discussing the ERE Life events, *birth, death, injury, marriage, divorce,* etc., and FrameNet is again proving to be inspirational. SemLink+ will encompass our growing Event Ontology, as well as the mappings between the resources and the multiple layers of annotation on the same data.

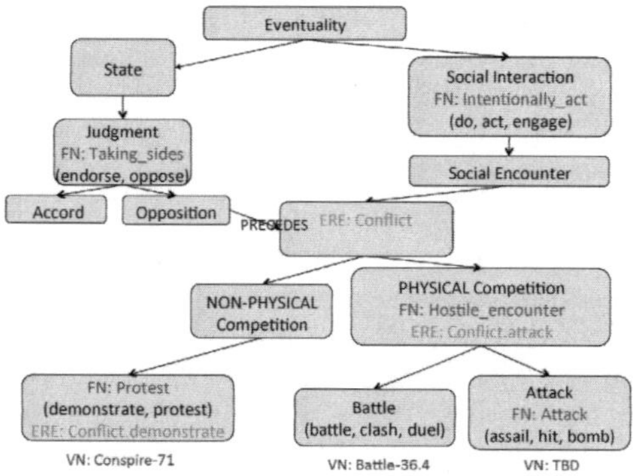


**Figure 1 – SemLink+ Event Ontology, partial**

## 5 Conclusion

Since computers do not interact with and experience the world the same way humans do, how could they ever interpret language describing the world the same way humans do? That NLP has made as much progress as it has is truly phenomenal, and there is much more still that can be done. Rich, detailed, lexical resources like FrameNet are major stepping stones that will enable continued improvements in the automatic representation of sentences in context. FrameNet, and WordNet, PropBank, VerbNet and SemLink+, provide priceless, invaluable information about myriads of different types of events and the creative ways in which they can be expressed, as well as rich details about all of their possible participants. If we can harness the power of distributional semantics to help us dynamically extend and enrich what has already been manually created, we may find our computers to be much smarter than we ever imagined them to be.


## Acknowledgments

This work has benefited immensely from comments and suggestions during the discussions of the RED working group on Event Ontologies, especially from Teruko Mitamura, Annie Zaenen, Ann Bies, and German Rigau. We also gratefully acknowledge the support of the National Science Foundation Grant NSF-IIS-1116782, A Bayesian Approach to Dynamic Lexical Resources for Flexible Language Processing, DARPA FA-8750-13-2-0045, subaward 560215 (via LDC) DEFT: Deep Exploration and Filtering of Text, DARPA Machine Reading (via BBN), and NIH: 1 R01 LM010090-01A1, THYME, (via Harvard). The content is solely the responsibility of the authors and does not necessarily represent the official views of DARPA, NSF or NIH.


## References


Daniel Bauer & Owen Rambow, 2011, Increasing Coverage of Syntactic Subcategorization Patterns in FrameNet Using VerbNet, In the *Proceedings of the IEEE Fifth International Conference on Semantic Computing.*

Claire Bonial, Julia Bonn, Kathryn Conger, Jena Hwang and Martha Palmer, 2014. PropBank: Semantics of New Predicate Types. The *9th edition of the Language Resources and Evaluation Conference.* Reykjavik, Iceland.

Claire Bonial, Kevin, Stowe, and Martha Palmer, 2013. Renewing and Revising SemLink. *The GenLex Workshop on Linked Data in Linguistics,* held with GenLex-13.

Dipanjan Das, Nathan Schneider, Desai Chen, and Noah A. Smith, 2010. Probabilistic Frame-Semantic Parsing. In *Proceedings of the NAACL 2010.*

David Dowty, 1991. Thematic Proto-Roles and Argument Selection. *Language*, 67:547-619

Christiane Fellbaum, 1998. *WordNet: An Electronic Lexical Data-base.* Language, Speech and Communications. MIT Press

Charles. J. Fillmore; Collin F. Baker, and H. Sato, 2004. FrameNet as a ``Net". In *Proceedings of LREC* 2004, *4*, pages 1091-1094

Charles J. Fillmore, Russell R. Lee-Goldman, and Russell Rhodes. 2012. "The FrameNet Constructicon" Boas, H.C. and Sag, I.A. (Eds.) *Sign-based Construction Grammar*, CSLI Publications.

Ana-Maria Guiglea and Alessandro Moschitti. 2006. Semantic role labeling via FrameNet, VerbNet and PropBank. In Proceedings of Coling-ACL 2006, pages 929–936.

Rei Ikuta and Martha Palmer (2014) Challenges of Adding Causation to Richer Event Descriptions, *In the Proceedings of 2nd Events Workshop, held with ACL 2014,* Baltimore, MD.

Karin Kipper, Anna Korhonen, Neville Ryant and Martha Palmer. 2008. A Large-Scale Classification of English Verbs. *Language Resources and Evaluation Journal, 42(1):21–40*

Maddalen Lopez de Lacalle, Egoitz Laparra, German Rigau, 2014, Predicate Matrix: extending SemLink throughWordNet mappings, The *9th edition of the Language Resources and Evaluation Conference.* Reykjavik, Iceland.

Ian Niles and Adam Pease, 2001. Towards a Standard Upper Ontology. In *Proceedings of the 2nd International Conference on Formal Ontology in Information Systems (FOIS-2001),* Chris Welty and Barry Smith, eds, Ogunquit, Maine, October 17-19, 2001.

Paola Merlo and Lonneke van der Plas. 2009. Abstraction and generalization in semantic role labels: PropBank, VerbNet or both?, In the *Proceedings of ACL 2009.*

Martha Palmer, 2009. SemLink: Linking PropBank, VerbNet and FrameNet, *In the Proceedings of the Generative Lexicon Conference, GenLex-09.*

Martha Palmer, Daniel Gildea, and Paul Kingsbury. 2005. The Proposition Bank: An Annotated Corpus of Semantic Roles. *Computational Linguistics, 31(1):71–106*

Martha Palmer, Daniel Gildea and Nianwen Xue. Semantic Role Labeling. 2010. Synthesis Lectures on Human Language Technology Series, ed. Graeme Hirst, Morgan and Claypoole.

Ralph Weischedel, Eduard Hovy, Mitchell Marcus, Martha Palmer, Robert Belvin, Sameer Pradan, Lance Ramshaw and Nianwen Xue. OntoNotes: A Large Training Corpus for Enhanced Processing, included in Part 1 : Data Acquisition and Linguistic Resources of the *Handbook of Natural Language Processing and Machine Translation: Global Automatic Language Exploitation* Editors: Joseph Olive, Caitlin Christianson, John McCary, Springer Verglag, pp 54-63, 201

# FrameNet and Linked Data

**Nancy Ide**
Department of Computer Science, Vassar College
Poughkeepsie, New York USA
ide@cs.vassar.edu

## Abstract

FrameNet is the ideal resource for representation as linked data, and several renderings of the resource in RDF/OWL have been created. FrameNet has also been and continues to be linked to other major resources, including WordNet, BabelNet, and MASC, in the Linguistic Linked Open Data cloud. Although so far the supporting technologies have not enabled easy and widespread access to the envisioned massive network of language resources, a conflation of recent efforts suggests this may be a reality in the not-too-distant future.

FrameNet (Fillmore et al., 2002; Ruppenhofer et al., 2006) is the ideal resource for representation in the Semantic Web (SW) as what is now widely known as "linked data". The Semantic Web consists of objects whose properties are represented by named links to other objects that constitute their values and supports representing and reasoning over ontologies defined the the SW framework. FrameNet is also a complex semantic network linking lexical units to semantic frames, and semantic frames to one another in a shallow hierarchy, over which inheritance and sub-frame relations are defined. In sentences annotated for FrameNet frame elements, the role is a property of a frame object that is linked to the entity (object) that fills it; FrameNet also includes a hierarchy of semantic types that constrain the possible fillers for a given role. FrameNet thus defines a dense network of objects and properties supported by ontological relations–exactly what the Semantic Web is intended to be.[1]

The suitability of FrameNet for representation in the Semantic Web was recognized fairly early on in the development of the family of Semantic Web formats, which include the Resource Definition Framework (RDF) and the Web Ontology Language (OWL), which first became available as W3C standards in the late 90s and early 2000s. In one of the earliest projects to adapt linguistic resources to the Semantic Web, FrameNet was rendered in RDF and DAML+OIL (the precursor to OWL) in 2003, soon after these formats first became standardized, for the stated goal of providing "a potential resource to aid in the automatic identification and disambiguation of word meanings on the semantic web" (Narayanan et al., 2003a). Later, the DAML+OIL portion was converted to OWL (Scheffczyk et al., 2008; Scheffczyk et al., 2010). Other conversions include (Coppola et al., 2009) and (Narayanan et al., 2003b); most recently, FrameNet was ported to RDF/OWL for inclusion in the Linked Open Data (LOD) cloud[2] (Nuzzolese et al., 2011). The possibility of linking WordNet and FrameNet in the Semantic Web has also spawned efforts such as (Bryl et al., 2012) that build on numerous efforts over the past several years to align and/or extend these two resources (Burchardt et al., 2005; Ide, 2006; De Cao et al., 2008; de Melo et al., 2012; Bryl et al., 2012). Others have analyzed FrameNet in order to formalize its semantics so as to be appropriate for use with Description Logic (DL) reasoners compatible with OWL-DL (Ovchinnikova et al., 2010).

Given all of the activity surrounding FrameNet as a resource for the Semantic Web, one would expect to see multiple examples of the use of Semantic Web implementations of FrameNet for NLP development and research. However, these examples do not exist, for two reasons. The first is a reality of the Semantic Web: simply put, the Semantic Web has not yet come to fruition, despite its having been around as a concept for well over a decade, and despite the development of a suite of W3C standard technologies to support it.

[1] For a fuller description of the structure of FrameNet data, see (Scheffczyk et al., 2008).

[2] http://linkeddata.org



*Proceedings of Frame Semantics in NLP: A Workshop in Honor of Chuck Fillmore (1929–2014)*, pages 18–21,
Baltimore, Maryland USA, June 27, 2014. ©2014 Association for Computational Linguistics

One of the most important of these technologies is SPARQL (Prud'hommeaux and Seaborne, 2008), a query language for data in RDF format, which is the crucial tool for exploiting the inter-linkages among linguistic resources to support NLP. Unfortunately, SPARQL is new enough that it is not yet widely deployed and has not had the benefit of decades of optimization to improve its performance, which so far often suffers from sluggishness. The good news is that new research and implementations are rapidly contributing to the improvement of SPARQL and other Semantic Web technologies, and as a result, we are seeing signs that the requisite base infrastructure may be (or may soon be) in place to support accelerated growth and deployment.

At the same time, over the past four or five years several efforts in Semantic Web development–in particular, the deployment of knowledge bases, lexicons, ontologies, and similar resources as linked data–have made notable progress, including the LOD cloud and, of special interest for the NLP community, its companion Linguistic Linked Open Data (LLOD) cloud (Chiarcos et al., 2012a). Efforts to link, especially, lexical-semantic databases like FrameNet, WordNet, and BabelNet (Navigli and Ponzetto, 2010) are underway, although full, operational linkage may not be immediate. At the same time, however, there is virtually no language *data* in the form of corpora in the LLOD, and none that contains annotations that can be linked to lexicons and knowledge bases.

This suggests a second reason why FrameNet as linked data has not yet been used in NLP research: a more useful configuration for a FrameNet-based resource in the Semantic Web would include linkage from frame governors and frame elements to (many) examples in corpora, rather than a simple rendering of linkages among lexical units, frames, and frame elements. Coupled with linkage to WordNet and multilingual semantic resources such as BabelNet (which has also been recently ported to RDF–see (Navigli, 2012)), a Semantic Web resource of this type and magnitude would enable SPARQL queries that collect information across several linguistic phenomena and levels, for example, "find all tokens in English and Russian that refer to *land* as a political unit (synonyms from the WordNet synset land%1:15:02::) in the VICTIM role of the ATTACK frame". This is a trivial example; the full range of possibilities is left to the reader's imagination, and awaits SPARQL's transition to full adulthood.

FrameNet has always hand-annotated sample sentences as input to frame construction, due to the insistence by FrameNet's founder on grounding the theory in real language data. FrameNet's early annotation efforts used examples from the British National Corpus (BNC); however, as time went on, FrameNet and similar annotation projects[3] found that usage examples extracted from the BNC were often unusable or misrepresentative for developing templates to describe semantic arguments and the like, due to significant syntactic differences between British and American English. This motivated a proposal for an American National Corpus (ANC)[4] (Fillmore et al., 1998), comparable to the BNC but including genres non-existent at the time of BNC development (blogs, email, chat rooms, tweets, etc.) as well as annotations beyond part-of-speech, to serve as basis for the development of lexical-semantic resources and NLP research in general.[5]

In 2006, the ANC, FrameNet, and WordNet projects received a substantial grant from the U.S. National Science Foundation[6] to produce a half-million word Manually Annotated Sub-Corpus (MASC)[7] (Ide et al., 2010), consisting of data drawn from the ANC and annotated for multiple types of linguistic phenomena. The project included a component to annotate portions of the corpus for WordNet senses and FrameNet frame elements, in order to provide input to an effort to harmonize these two resources (Baker and Fellbaum, 2009). The first full version of the corpus, released in 2012, included over 16 different annotation types and was coupled with a separate sentence corpus (Passonneau et al., 2012) that includes WordNet 3.1 sense-tags for approximately 1000 occurrences of each of 114 words chosen by the WordNet and FrameNet teams (ca. 114,000 annotated occurrences). Of these, 100 occurrences of each word (over 1000 sentences) are also anno-

[3]E.g., Comlex (http://nlp.cs.nyu.edu/comlex/) and NomLex (http://nlp.cs.nyu.edu/nomlex/)

[4]http://www.anc.org/

[5]The ANC never received the substantial funding and text contributions enjoyed by the BNC, and as a result has so far released only 22 million words of data, including a 15 million word subset that is unrestricted for any use called the Open ANC" (OANC), available at http://www.anc.org/data/oanc/.

[6]NSF CRI 0708952

[7]http://www.anc.org/data/masc/

tated for FrameNet frame elements. These annotations were subsequently used in a major WordNet-FrameNet alignment effort (de Melo et al., 2012).

MASC provides a missing link in the Semantic Web scenario for FrameNet and related resources. The corpus contains not only FrameNet and WordNet annotations, but also annotations over parts or all the corpus at several other linguistic layers including morphosyntax, syntax (shallow parse, Penn Treebank annotation), semantics (named entities, opinion, PropBank), and discourse (coreference, clause boundaries and nucleus/satellite relations). All of MASC is currently being incorporated into the LLOD cloud, and its FrameNet and WordNet annotations will be linked to the linked data versions of those resources.[8] The resulting resource, connecting multiple major semantic resources and a broad-genre corpus, will be unparalleled as a foundation for NLP research and development.

When the annotations for other phenomena in MASC are added into the mix, the potential to study and process language data *across* multiple linguistic levels becomes even greater. It is increasingly recognized that to perform human-like language understanding, NLP systems will ultimately have to dynamically integrate information from all linguistic levels as they process input, but despite this recognition most work in the field continues to focus on isolated phenomena or utilizes only selected phenomena from a few linguistic levels. Some corpora with multiple annotation layers, including MASC and a (very few) others such as OntoNotes (Pradhan et al., 2007), have recently been created, but due to the high costs of their development they are limited in size and do not include annotations across the gamut of linguistic phenomena. Similarly, standardized formats for annotated data (e.g., (ISO, 2012)), lexical-semantic resources (ISO, 2008), and reference categories for linguistic annotations (Marc Kemps-Snijders and Wright, 2008) have been developed to enable merging of annotations of different types and formats, but there still remains considerable disparity among and/or lack of support for processing merged resources.

[8] See (Chiarcos et al., 2012b) for a discussion of the process and benefits. BabelNet annotations of MASC, which are in turn linked to wordnets in multiple languages, have also been recently contributed (Moro et al., 2014), thus opening up the possibility for linkage from MASC to that resource as well–and, by extension, linkage between BabelNet and MASC's existing FrameNet and WordNet annotations.

Is the Semantic Web the answer? Will it be the vehicle for a paradigm shift in NLP research and development? Likely, it or something it evolves into will ultimately provide the required common representation and processing framework which, coupled with potentially enormous advances in computer and network speed, data capacity, neurotechnology, network-on-chip technologies, and the like, will fundamentally change our approach to NLP in the decades to come. In the meantime, it remains to be seen how quickly Semantic Web technology will progress, and how soon most or all language resources will reside in places like the LLOD cloud, so that they can begin to be fully and readily exploited. But whether the Semantic Web as we know it now is the ultimate solution or simply a developmental step, the direction seems clear; and fittingly, FrameNet is one of the first resources on board.

## References

Collin F. Baker and Christiane Fellbaum. 2009. WordNet and FrameNet as Complementary Resources for Annotation. In *Proceedings of the Third Linguistic Annotation Workshop*, pages 125–129.

Volha Bryl, Sara Tonelli, Claudio Giuliano, and Luciano Serafini. 2012. A novel Framenet-based resource for the semantic web. In *SAC*, pages 360–365.

Aljoscha Burchardt, Katrin Erk, and Anette Frank. 2005. A WordNet detour to FrameNet. In *Proceedings of the GLDV 2005 workshop GermaNet II*.

Christian Chiarcos, Sebastian Hellmann, and Sebastian Nordhoff. 2012a. Linking Linguistic Resources: Examples from the Open Linguistics Working Group. In *Linked Data in Linguistics*, pages 201–216. Springer.

Christian Chiarcos, John McCrae, Philipp Cimiano, and Christiane Fellbaum. 2012b. Towards open data for linguistics: Linguistic linked data. In *New Trends of Research in Ontologies and Lexical Resources*. Springer.

Bonaventura Coppola, Aldo Gangemi, Alfio Massimiliano Gliozzo, Davide Picca, and Valentina Presutti. 2009. Frame Detection over the Semantic Web. In *Proceedings of the 6th European Semantic Web Conference*.

Diego De Cao, Danilo Croce, Marco Pennacchiotti, and Roberto Basili. 2008. Combining Word Sense and Usage for Modeling Frame Semantics. In *Proceedings of the 2008 Conference on Semantics in Text Processing*, pages 85–101.

Gerard de Melo, Collin F. Baker, Nancy Ide, Rebecca Passonneau, and Christiane Fellbaum. 2012. Empirical Comparisons of MASC Word Sense Annotations. In *Eighth International Conference on Language Resources and Evaluation (LREC 2012)*.

Charles J. Fillmore, Nancy Ide, Daniel Jurafsky, and Catherine Macleod. 1998. An American National Corpus: A Proposal. In *Proceedings of the First Annual Conference on Language Resources and Evaluation*, pages 965–969, Granada, Spain.

Charles J. Fillmore, Collin F. Baker, and Hiroaki Sato. 2002. The FrameNet Database and Software Tools. In *Proceedings of the Third International Conference on Language Resources and Evaluation*, volume IV.

Nancy Ide, Collin Baker, Christiane Fellbaum, and Rebecca Passonneau. 2010. The Manually Annotated Sub-Corpus: A Community Resource for and by the People. In *Proceedings of ACL 2010*, pages 68–73.

Nancy Ide. 2006. Making Senses: Bootstrapping Sense-Tagged Lists of Semantically-Related Words. In *Computational Linguistics and Intelligent Text*, pages 13–27.

2008. Language Resource Management – Lexical Markup Framework. International Standard ISO 24613.

2012. Language Resource Management – Linguistic Annotation Framework. International Standard ISO 24612.

Peter Wittenburg Marc Kemps-Snijders, Menzo Windhouwer and Sue Ellen Wright. 2008. ISOCat: Corralling Data Categories in the Wild. In *Proceedings of the Sixth International Conference on Language Resources and Evaluation (LREC'08)*.

Andrea Moro, Roberto Navigli, Francesco Maria Tucci, and Rebecca J. Passonneau. 2014. Annotating the MASC corpus with babelnet. In *Proceedings of the Ninth International Conference on Language Resources and Evaluation (LREC' 2014)*.

Srini Narayanan, Collin F. Baker, Charles J. Fillmore, and Miriam R.L. Petruck. 2003a. FrameNet Meets the Semantic Web: Lexical Semantics for the Web. In *The Semantic Web - ISWC 2003*, pages 771–787. Springer.

Srinivas Narayanan, Miriam R.L. Petruck, Collin F. Baker, and Charles J. Fillmore. 2003b. Putting FrameNet Data into the ISO Linguistic Annotation Framework. In *Proceedings of the ACL 2003 Workshop on Linguistic Annotation: Getting the Model Right*, page 22–29.

Roberto Navigli and Simone Paolo Ponzetto. 2010. BabelNet: Building a Very Large Multilingual Semantic Network. In *Proceedings of the 48th Annual Meeting of the Association for Computational Linguistics*, pages 216–225.

Roberto Navigli. 2012. BabelNet goes to the (Multilingual) Semantic Web. In *ISWC 2012 Workshop on Multilingual Semantic Web*.

Andrea Giovanni Nuzzolese, Aldo Gangemi, and Valentina Presutti. 2011. Gathering lexical linked data and knowledge patterns from FrameNet. In *K-CAP*, pages 41–48.

Ekaterina Ovchinnikova, Laure Vieu, Alessandro Oltramari, Stefano Borgo, and Theodore Alexandrov. 2010. Data-Driven and Ontological Analysis of FrameNet for Natural Language Reasoning. In *Proceedings of the Seventh conference on International Language Resources and Evaluation (LREC'10)*.

Rebecca J. Passonneau, Collin F. Baker, Christiane Fellbaum, and Nancy Ide. 2012. The MASC Word Sense Corpus. In *Proceedings of the Eighth International Conference on Language Resources and Evaluation (LREC 2012)*.

Sameer S. Pradhan, Eduard H. Hovy, Mitchell P. Marcus, Martha Palmer, Lance A. Ramshaw, and Ralph M. Weischedel. 2007. Ontonotes: A unified relational semantic representation. In *Proceedings of the First IEEE International Conference on Semantic Computing (ICSC 2007)*, pages 517–526.

Eric Prud'hommeaux and Andy Seaborne. 2008. SPARQL Query Language for RDF.

Josef Ruppenhofer, Michael Ellsworth, Miriam R.L. Petruck, Christopher R. Johnson, and Jan Scheffczyk. 2006. *FrameNet II: Extended Theory and Practice*. International Computer Science Institute.

Jan Scheffczyk, Collin F. Baker, and Srini Narayanan. 2008. Ontology-Based reasoning about lexical resources. In *Ontologies and Lexical Resources for Natural Language Processing*. Cambridge University Press.

Jan Scheffczyk, Collin Baker, and Srrini Narayanan, 2010. *Reasoning over Natural Language Text by Means of FrameNet and Ontologies*, pages 53–71. Cambridge University Press.

# Bridging Text and Knowledge with Frames

**Srini Narayanan**
Google Zurich / Brandschenkestrasse 110, 8002 Zurich, Switzerland
snarayanan0@gmail.com

## Abstract

FrameNet is the best currently operational version of Chuck Fillmore's Frame Semantics. As FrameNet has evolved over the years, we have been building a series of increasingly ambitious prototype systems that exploit FrameNet as a semantic resource. Results from this work point to frames as a natural representation for applications that require linking textual meaning to world knowledge.

## 1 Introduction

Frame Semantics (Fillmore, 1976) defines the meaning of a word with respect to the conceptual structure (Frame) that it evokes. The promise of Frame Semantics is that it is a principled method to connect language analysis with concepts and knowledge. This paper summarizes over a decade of research at Berkeley[1] on computational models bridging text and inference using Frame Semantics. We will start with a brief description of the lexical resource, FrameNet[2], designed with the explicit goal to capturing insights and findings from Frame Semantics in an on-line lexicon. We then describe computational models that exploit the semantic information in FrameNet for a variety of NLP tasks.

## 2 FrameNet

The Berkeley FrameNet project (Fillmore, Johnson, & Petruck, 2003) is building a lexicon based on the theory of Frame Semantics. In FrameNet, the meanings of lexical items (lexical units (LU)) are defined with respect to larger structured representations, called Frames. Individual lexical units evoke specific frames and establish a binding pattern to specific slots or roles (frame elements (FE)) within the frame. FrameNet describes the underlying frames for different lexical units, examines sentences related to the frames using a very large corpus, and records (annotates) the ways in which information from the associated frames are expressed in these sentences. The result is a database that contains a set of frames (related through hierarchy and composition), a set of frame elements for each frame, and a set of frame annotated sentences that covers the different patterns of usage for lexical units in the frame. Collin Baker's paper in this conference has more details on the FrameNet project including the current state of the resource which is now available in multiple languages. This paper summarizes the results of applying FrameNet in a variety of NLP applications.

### 2.1 FrameNet data as seed patterns for Information Extraction

While FrameNet frames and FE tags are meaningful to human interpreters, they are not suitable for direct use in NLP applications. One early project explored using the FrameNet annotated dataset to automatically compile patterns and a lexicon for Information Extraction (IE) (Mohit and Narayanan, 2003). A distinguishing feature that made FrameNet attractive for this purpose was its explicit mandate to cover all the valence patterns for a target word, not just the frequent ones. Thus, FrameNet annotations and valence alternations were designed to capture the long tail for every target lexeme. We hypothesized that using a highly precise set of patterns and a lexicon automatically compiled from the FrameNet frame relational database and annotations should result good performance for the task. To increase coverage, we extended the frame lexicon with WordNet synsets. As a first test, we culled a set of news stories from Yahoo News Service with topics re-

[1] All the work described was done while the author was at the University of California, Berkeley and the International Computer Science Institute (ICSI) / 1947 Center Street, Berkeley CA 94704.

[2] http://framenet.icsi.berkeley.edu



*Proceedings of Frame Semantics in NLP: A Workshop in Honor of Chuck Fillmore (1929–2014)*, pages 22–25,
Baltimore, Maryland USA, June 27, 2014. ©2014 Association for Computational Linguistics

lated to the topic of *crime*. We also compiled a set of IE patterns and lexicon from several crime related frames (such as Arrest, Detain, Arraign and Verdict.) We were able to achieve an average precision of 76.5% and an average recall to 66% for the stories in this domain. However, the relatively sparse and uneven domain coverage of FrameNet and the absence of high quality parsers and named entity annotators (used for building expressive and general patterns) at the time made the pilot task difficult to repeat in an open domain setting. While the coverage of FrameNet is still an issue, the enormous gains made in the quality and amount of parsed and named entity annotated data could make this early work attractive again where FrameNet can be used as a high precision seed pattern generator in a semi-supervised IE setting.

## 3 From Frames to Inference

A fundamental aspect of Frame Semantics, one that directly connected the linguistic insights of Chuck Fillmore to the early work in AI by Schank, Abelson, Minsky, and others was the idea that Frames were central to how inferences were packaged. In this view, framing provided preferential access to specific *expected* inferences. These inferences were said to be *in the frame*. Schankian scripts (such as the famous restaurant script) (Schank and Abelson, 1977) are a good example of such inferential packaging in terms of expected sequences of events, participants, and outcomes. In addition to providing such general inferences, Chuck Fillmore observed that *linguistic framing* also provided a way to delineate multiple perspectives on an event (including foregrounding, backgrounding, and participant perspective). An example can be found in the perspective difference provided by the lexical items *sell*, *buy*, or *pay*, which all evoke the commercial transaction frame.

(Chang, Narayanan, & Petruck, 2002), built a computational formalism that captured structural frame relationships among participants in a dynamic scenario. This representation was used to describe the internal structure and relationships between FrameNet frames in terms of parameters for active event simulations for inference. We applied our formalism to the *commerce domain* and showed how it provides a flexible means of handling linguistic perspective and other challenges of semantic representation. While this work was able to computationally model subtle inferential effects in perspective and framing choice, it remains a proof of concept demonstration and there was a need to do an automatic translation to an inference formalism which would enable us to use more robust reasoners (the trade-off was of course that these off the shelf reasoners produced shallower inferences).

(Scheffczyk, Baker, & Narayanan, 2010) automatically translated a crucial portion of FrameNet to the description logic based web ontology language OWL, and showed how state-of-the-art description logic reasoners can make inferences over FrameNet-annotated sentences. Thus, annotated text becomes available to the Semantic Web and FrameNet itself can be linked to other ontologies. While our OWL translation is limited to facts included in FrameNet, links to ontologies make world knowledge available to reasoning about natural language. Therefore, are linked FrameNet to the Suggested Upper Merged Ontology (SUMO). This ground work gives a clear motivation for the design of further ontology bindings and defines the baseline for measuring their benefits.

Fillmore's further insights into the connections between textual inference and world knowledge led us to ask the question of how a linguistic analysis of a written document can contribute to identifying, tracking and populating the eventualities that are presented in the document, either directly or indirectly, and representing degrees of belief concerning them. This work, reported in (Fillmore, Narayanan, & Baker, 2006), attempts to clarify the boundary between on the one hand the information that can be derived on the basis of linguistic knowledge alone (composed of lexical meanings and the meanings of grammatical constructions) and on the other hand, reasoning based on beliefs about the source of a document, world knowledge, and common sense. In particular, we show that the kind of information produced by FrameNet can have a special role in contributing to text understanding, starting from the basic facts of the combinatorial properties of frame-bearing words (verbs, nouns, adjectives and prepositions) and arriving at the means of recognizing the anaphoric properties of specific unexpressed event participants. Framenet defines a new layer of anaphora resolution and text cohesion based on the annotations of the different types of null instantiations (Definite Null Instantiation (DNI), Indefinite Null Instantiation (INI), and Constructional Null

Instantiation (CNI)). A full exploitation of these linguistic signals in a coreference resolver is still pending.

## 4 Frame Semantics in Question Answering

As FrameNet matured, we started asking if it could be used for semantically based question answering for questions that went beyond factoids and required deeper semantic information. (Narayanan and Harabagiu, 2004; Sinha and Narayanan, 2005; Sinha, 2008) report on a prototype question answering system that attempted to answer questions related to causality, event structure, and temporality in specific domains. The project on Question Answering (QA) was a joint effort with Sanda Harabagiu's group at UT Dallas.

The QA work was based on the fact that events, while independent of language themselves, are frequently discussed in natural language, yielding copious data in that form. To reason about complex events requires an interface from event models to data sources. We sought to exploit semantic frames as an intermediate structure and interface between event descriptions in natural language and event models that produce inferences to answer questions. In the course of this project, we came up with the basic framework and algorithms combining a variety of NLP techniques including Parsing, Topic Modeling, Named Entity Recognition, and Semantic Role Labeling with deep event structure inference in multiple domains. The frame structure in language provides a bi-directional mapping from language to event models, enabling us to link information found in text about an event of interest to models that represent that event. The proof of concept system used frame parsed input with a set of hand built domain ontologies for specific domains. The system was able to answer domain questions involving causal, diagnostic, and hypothetical reasoning. While the results clearly showed the utility of FrameNet as a resource supporting deep semantic inference, it also delineated the necessity and role of domain specific ontologies and inference required to realize an end-to-end system using FrameNet.

## 5 Frames, Constructions and Grammar

Yet another of Fillmore's profound insights was the observation that every unit of grammar is most effectively described as a pairing between form and meaning, aka a construction. Constructions exist at lexical (and sub-lexical) levels as well as at larger granularities (phrases, discourse) playing a crucial role in the compositionally of language. This proposal, entitled construction grammar, has gained considerable empirical support in large part due to the investigations of Fillmore, his colleagues and students, reported in a series of beautiful papers on the grammatical and compositional properties of constructions.[3]

Research on construction grammar has played a fundamental role within our Berkeley interdisciplinary project, NTL[4], which is attempting to build cognitively plausible computational models of language acquisition and use. Specifically, NTL research has resulted in the grammar formalism called Embodied Construction Grammar (ECG), where the meaning pole of a construction is expressed in terms of bindings between bodily schemas (also called Image Schemas) and frames. ECG allows constraints of all kinds (phonological, syntactic, semantic, etc.) in a unification based probabilistic framework, where the best fitting interpretation in context is selected as the analysis of the input. ECG is formally defined and computationally implemented, and has been used for linguistic analysis, in models of language comprehension, and for cognitive models of language learning[5].

## 6 Frame Semantics and Metaphor

FrameNet has long held the goal of including information about metaphorical usage in language. The most recent project on Frame Semantics is the ICSI MetaNet project, where the goal is to build a system that extracts linguistic manifestations of metaphor (words and phrases that are based on metaphor) from text and interprets them automatically in four different languages.

The MetaNet project, is a multi-lingual, multi-university, multi-disciplinary effort that incorporates FN methodology as well as corpus and machine learning techniques, deep cognitive linguistics, and behavioral and imaging experiments.

MetaNet models metaphor as a mapping between two different frames. Such mappings

[3] `http://www.constructiongrammar.org/` is a currently active resource on the topic with contributions from a variety of international scholars.

[4] `http://ntl.icsi.berkeley.edu/ntl`

[5] `http://ecgweb.pbworks.com/w/page/15044343/FrontPage`

project information from a source frame to a target frame. The information projected is partial and can include the frame, its slots, and filler constraints. An initial repository of mappings that draws on FrameNet frames as sources and targets of the mappings is used as base information by a system that extracts additional metaphors using machine learning. The system uses what it has learned about the relationships between the frame elements of conceptual metaphors to find new metaphors in text. The MetaNet Wiki[6] is a database of such mappings, drawing on FrameNet's inventory of Frames. The mappings currently exist in four different languages. FrameNet frames and mappings constrain the search for new metaphors, and the discovery of new metaphors by a corpus based machine learning algorithm both a) provides empirical support for the existing frames and mappings and b) more importantly potentially extends the set by identifying gaps and inconsistencies in coverage. This interaction facilitates an iterative design process in MetaNet which is empirically driven and usage based, just as Fillmore would have insisted.[7]

## 7 Conclusion and Future Directions

Frame semantics in general and FrameNet in particular show considerable promise for use in deep semantic analysis. FrameNet frames are intended to capture crucial generalizations not available in other lexical resources. Various prototype systems have clearly demonstrated the potential of FrameNet to make a qualitative difference in semantic NLP. There remain two crucial gaps that have to be bridged. One is the issue of coverage. The second is the lack of a formal representation covering the more subtle inferential aspects of FrameNet. Progress is being made of both fronts as is evidenced in some of the papers in this workshop. If successful, the next few years should see an increasing use and acceptance of FrameNet as a crucial semantic resource bridging language analysis with inference. This will lead to scalable versions of the systems described in this paper, but will also give rise to new applications. One particularly intriguing area of research is the use of frames for cross-modal semantic representation bridging text, speech, and vision.

[6]`http://metaphor.icsi.berkeley.edu`

[7]Even at 83, Chuck's brilliant attention to detail and infectious enthusiasm fundamentally shaped the early MetaNet project on a day-to-day basis, till his illness sadly made direct participation impossible after 2012.

## Acknowledgments

All the projects described here were collaborations with the FrameNet and NTL groups at ICSI and Berkeley. This line of inquiry will continue to be dedicated to and guided by Chuck Fillmore's invaluable insights, vision, and body of work.

## References

Nancy Chang, Srini Narayanan, and Miriam R. L. Petruck. 2002. Putting Frames in Perspective. *Proceedings of 19th International Conference on Computational Linguistics. Taipei*: COLING, 2002.

Charles Fillmore. 1976. Frame semantics and the nature of language. *Annals of the New York Academy of Sciences: Conference on the Origin and Development of Language and Speech*, 280, 1,20-32, 1976.

Charles Fillmore, Christopher R. Johnson, and Miriam R. L. Petruck. 2003. Background to FrameNet. *International Journal of Lexicography*. 16.3 (2003): 235-250.

Charles Fillmore, Srini Narayanan, Collin Baker. 2006. What Linguistics can contribute to Event Extraction. AAAI Workshop on Event Extraction, AAAI 2006, Boston.

Behrang Mohit and Srini Narayanan. 2003. *Semantic Extraction from Wide-Coverage Lexical Resources*, HLT-NAACL, Short Papers, 2003.

Srini Narayanan and Sanda Harabagiu 2004. Question Answering based on Semantic Structures. *International Conference on Computational Linguistics* (COLING 2004), Geneva, Switzerland, August 22-29, 2004.

Roger Schank and Robert P. Abelson. 1977 *Scripts, plans, goals and understanding: An inquiry into human knowledge structures*, Erlbaum, 1977. ISBN 0-470-99033-3.

Jan Scheffczyk, Collin F. Baker, Srini Narayanan. 2010. Reasoning over Natural Language Text by Means of FrameNet and Ontologies. *Ontology and the Lexicon: A Natural Language Processing Perspective*. Eds. Chu-ren Huang, et al. Studies in Natural Language Processing. Cambridge, UK: Cambridge University Press, 2010. 53-71.

Steve Sinha and Srini Narayanan. 2005. Model Based Answer Selection. Textual Inference in Question Answering Workshop, AAAI 2005, Pittsburgh, July 2005.

Steven Sinha. 2008. *Answering Questions about Complex Events* PhD Dissertation, Department of EECS, Berkeley, CA, 2008.

# Statistical Models for Frame-Semantic Parsing

**Dipanjan Das**
Google Inc.
76 9th Avenue,
New York, NY 10011
dipanjand@google.com

## Abstract

We present a brief history and overview of statistical methods in frame-semantic parsing – the automatic analysis of text using the theory of frame semantics. We discuss how the FrameNet lexicon and frame-annotated datasets have been used by statistical NLP researchers to build usable, state-of-the-art systems. We also focus on future directions in frame-semantic parsing research, and discuss NLP applications that could benefit from this line of work.

## 1 Frame-Semantic Parsing

Frame-semantic parsing has been considered as the task of automatically finding semantically salient **targets** in text, disambiguating their semantic **frame** representing an event and scenario in discourse, and annotating arguments consisting of words or phrases in text with various frame elements (or **roles**). The FrameNet lexicon (Baker et al., 1998), an ontology inspired by the theory of frame semantics (Fillmore, 1982), serves as a repository of semantic frames and their roles. Figure 1 depicts a sentence with three evoked frames for the targets "million", "created" and "pushed" with FrameNet frames and roles.

Automatic analysis of text using frame-semantic structures can be traced back to the pioneering work of Gildea and Jurafsky (2002). Although their experimental setup relied on a primitive version of FrameNet and only made use of "exemplars" or example usages of semantic frames (containing one target per sentence) as opposed to a "corpus" of sentences, it resulted in a flurry of work in the area of automatic semantic role labeling (Màrquez et al., 2008). However, the focus of semantic role labeling (SRL) research has mostly been on PropBank (Palmer et al., 2005) conventions, where verbal targets could evoke a "sense" frame, which is not shared across targets, making the frame disambiguation setup different from the representation in FrameNet. Furthermore, it is fair to say that early research on PropBank focused primarily on argument structure prediction, and the interaction between frame and argument structure analysis has mostly been unaddressed (Màrquez et al., 2008). There are exceptions, where the verb frame has been taken into account during SRL (Meza-Ruiz and Riedel, 2009; Watanabe et al., 2010). Moreoever, the CoNLL 2008 and 2009 shared tasks also include the verb and noun frame identification task in their evaluations, although the overall goal was to predict semantic dependencies based on PropBank, and not full argument spans (Surdeanu et al., 2008; Hajič et al., 2009).

The SemEval 2007 shared task (Baker et al., 2007) attempted to revisit the frame-semantic analysis task based on FrameNet. It introduced a larger FrameNet lexicon (version 1.3), and also a larger corpus with full-text annotations compared to prior work, with multiple targets annotated per sentence. The corpus allowed words and phrases with noun, verb, adjective, adverb, number, determiner, conjunction and preposition syntactic categories to serve as targets and evoke frames, unlike any other single dataset; it also allowed targets from different syntactic categories share frames, and therefore roles. The repository of semantic role types was also much richer than PropBank-style lexicons, numbering in several hundreds.

Most systems participating in the task resorted to a cascade of classifiers and rule-based modules: identifying targets (a non-trivial subtask), disambiguating frames, identifying potential arguments, and then labeling them with roles. The system described by Johansson and Nugues (2007) performed the best in this shared task. Next, we focus on its performance, and subsequent improvements made by the research community on this task.



*Proceedings of Frame Semantics in NLP: A Workshop in Honor of Chuck Fillmore (1929–2014)*, pages 26–29,
Baltimore, Maryland USA, June 27, 2014. ©2014 Association for Computational Linguistics

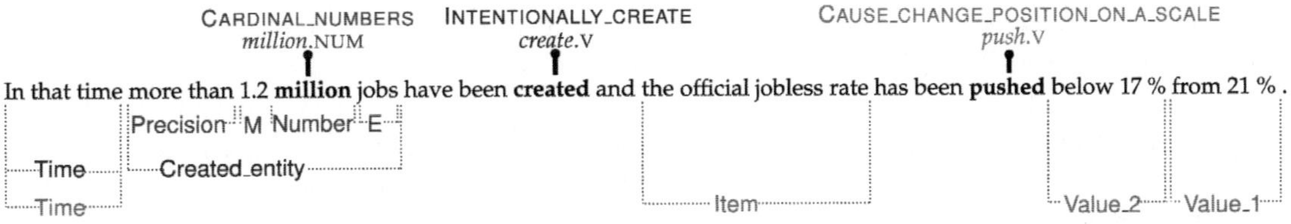


Figure 1: A partial depiction of frame-semantic structures taken from Das et al. (2014). The words in bold correspond to targets, which evoke semantic frames that are denoted in capital letters. Above each target is shown the corresponding lexical unit, which is a lemma appended by a coarse part-of-speech tag. Every frame is shown in a distinct color; each frame's arguments are annotated with the same color, and are marked below the sentence, at different levels. For the CARDINAL_NUMBERS frame, "M" denotes the role Multiplier and "E" denotes the role Entity.

| | | $P$ | $R$ | $F_1$ |
|---|---|---|---|---|
| **SemEval'07 Data** (automatic targets) | Johansson and Nugues (2007) | 51.59 | 35.44 | 42.01 |
| | Das et al. (2010) | **58.08** | **38.76** | **46.49** |
| **FrameNet 1.5 Release** (gold targets) | Das et al. (2014) | 68.33 | 61.14 | 64.54 |
| | Hermann et al. (2014) | **72.79** | **64.95** | **68.64** |

Table 1: We show the current state of the art on the frame-semantic parsing task. The first section shows results on the SemEval 2007 shared task. The best system in the task, presented by Johansson and Nugues (2007) was later outperformed by SEMAFOR, a system described by Das et al. (2010). Both systems use a rule-based module to identify targets. On the FrameNet 1.5 data, Das et al. (2014) presented additional semi-supervised experiments using gold targets, which was recently outperformed by an approach presented by Hermann et al. (2014) that made use of distributed word representations.

## 2 Current State of the Art

Johansson and Nugues (2007) presented the system that resulted in the best $F_1$ score on the SemEval 2007 task of collectively identifying frame-evoking targets, a disambiguated frame for each target, and the set of role-labeled arguments for each frame. The system contained a set of rule-based heuristics to identify targets followed by a cascade of three learned models as mentioned in §1. Das et al. (2010) presented a tool called SEMAFOR,[1] which improved upon this system with a similar framework for target identification, but only used two probabilistic models, one for frame identification, and one for predicting the arguments. The frame identification subpart involved a latent-variable log-linear model, which intended to capture frames for unseen targets, many of which appeared in the test data. Moreover, the feature sets in both the models were sufficiently different from prior work, resulting in improvements. Table 1 shows results on the SemEval 2007 data for these two systems.

The FrameNet project released more annotations and a larger frame lexicon in 2010; Das et al. (2014) used this dataset, and presented a variety of experiments improving upon their prior work, setting the new state of the art. A few salient aspects of this updated version of SEMAFOR involved handling unseen targets using a graph-based semi-supervised learning approach and improved inference using a dual decomposition algorithm. Subsequently, Hermann et al. (2014) used a very similar framework but presented a novel method using distributed word representations for better frame identification, outperforming the aforementioned update to SEMAFOR. Table 1 shows the performance in terms of $F_1$ score for frames and arguments given gold targets. Recent work on the FrameNet corpora, including the aforementioned two papers have used gold targets to measure the performance of statistical methods because the distribution of annotated targets in the data varied significantly across documents and domains, making it difficult to build a learnable system for target identification.

The aforementioned papers focused on the task of sentence-internal frame-semantic analysis. There have been some investigation of finding implicit arguments of frames that may be present in other parts of a document, outside the sentential context. Although there has not been extensive research on this topic, a shared task at SemEval 2010 focused on this problem (Ruppenhofer et al., 2010).[2] Moreover, there has been significant effort

[1] See http://www.ark.cs.cmu.edu/SEMAFOR.

[2] Related work on the analysis of implicit arguments for

in developing unsupervised techniques for inducing frame-semantic structures (Modi et al., 2012), to induce FrameNet-like lexicons from weak supervision, such as syntactic parses.

## 3 Applications

Shallow semantic analysis based on FrameNet data has been recently utilized across various natural language processing applications with success. These include the generation of meeting summaries (Kleinbauer, 2012), the prediction of stock price movement using (Xie et al., 2013), inducing slots for domain-specific dialog systems (Chen et al., 2013), stance classification in debates (Hasan and Ng, 2013), modeling the clarity of student essays (Persing and Ng, 2013) to name a few.

There is strong potential in using frame-semantic structures in other applications such as question answering and machine translation, as demonstrated by prior work using PropBank-style SRL annotations (Shen and Lapata, 2007; Liu and Gildea, 2010).

## 4 Future Directions

Given the wide body of work in frame-semantic analysis of text, and recent interest in using frame-semantic parsers in NLP applications, the future directions of research look exciting.

First and foremost, to improve the quality of automatic frame-semantic parsers, the coverage of the FrameNet lexicon on free English text, and the number of annotated targets needs to increase. For example, the training dataset used for the state-of-the-art system of Hermann et al. (2014) contains only 4,458 labeled targets, which is approximately 40 times less than the number of annotated targets in Ontonotes 4.0 (Hovy et al., 2006), a standard NLP dataset, containing PropBank-style verb annotations. This comparison is important because FrameNet covers many more syntactic categories than the PropBank-style annotations, and features more than 1,000 semantic role labels compared to 51 in Ontonotes, but severely lacks annotations. A machine learned system would find it very hard to generalize to new data given such data sparsity. Increasing the quantity of such annotations requires exhaustive inter-annotator agreement studies (which has been rare in FrameNet corpora generation) and the development of annotation guidelines, such that these annotations can be produced outside the FrameNet project.

Other than increasing the amount of labeled data, there is a necessity of automatically aligning predicate-level semantic knowledge present in resources like FrameNet, PropBank, NomBank and VerbNet (Schuler, 2005). These lexicons share a lot of knowledge about predicates and current resources like Ontonotes do align some of the information, but a lot remains missing. For example, alignment between these lexicons could be done within a statistical model for frame-semantic parsing, such that correlations between the coarse semantic role labels in PropBank or NomBank and the finer labels in FrameNet could be discovered automatically.

Finally, the FrameNet data is an attractive test bed for semi-supervised learning techniques because of data sparsity; distributed word representations, which often capture more semantic information than surface-form features could be exploited in various aspects of the frame-semantic parsing task.

nominal targets in NomBank (Meyers et al., 2004) has been investigated recently (Gerber and Chai, 2012).

## Acknowledgments

The author thanks Desai Chen, André Martins, Nathan Schneider and Noah Smith for numerous discussions and several years of collaboration on this topic at Carnegie Mellon. He is also grateful to Kuzman Ganchev, Oscar Täckström, Karl Moritz Hermann, Ryan McDonald, Slav Petrov, Fernando Pereira and the greater Research at Google community for helping research in this area thrive over the past couple of years.

## References

C. F. Baker, C. J. Fillmore, and J. B. Lowe. 1998. The Berkeley Framenet project. In *Proceedings of COLING-ACL.*

C. F. Baker, M. Ellsworth, and K. Erk. 2007. SemEval-2007 Task 19: Frame semantic structure extraction. In *Proceedings of SemEval.*

Y.-N. Chen, W. Y. Wang, and A. Rudnicky. 2013. Unsupervised induction and filling of semantic slots for spoken dialogue systems using frame-semantic parsing. In *Proceedings of ASRU.*

D. Das, N. Schneider, D. Chen, and N. A. Smith. 2010. Probabilistic frame-semantic parsing. In *Proceedings of NAACL-HLT.*

D. Das, D. Chen, A. F. T. Martins, N. Schneider, and N. A. Smith. 2014. Frame-semantic parsing. *Computational Linguistics*, 40(1):9–56.

C. J. Fillmore. 1982. Frame Semantics. In *Linguistics in the Morning Calm*, pages 111–137. Hanshin Publishing Co., Seoul, South Korea.

M. Gerber and J. Y. Chai. 2012. Semantic role labeling of implicit arguments for nominal predicates. *Computational Linguistics*, 38(4):755–798.

D. Gildea and D. Jurafsky. 2002. Automatic labeling of semantic roles. *Computational Linguistics*, 28(3):245–288.

J. Hajič, M. Ciaramita, R. Johansson, D. Kawahara, M. A. Martí, L. Màrquez, A. Meyers, J. Nivre, S. Padó, J. Štěpánek, P. Straňák, M. Surdeanu, N. Xue, and Y. Zhang. 2009. The CoNLL-2009 shared task: Syntactic and semantic dependencies in multiple languages. In *Proceedings of CoNLL*.

K. S. Hasan and V. Ng. 2013. Frame semantics for stance classification. In *Proceedings of CoNLL*.

K. M. Hermann, D. Das, J. Weston, and K. Ganchev. 2014. Semantic frame identification with distributed word representations. In *Proceedings of ACL*.

E. Hovy, M. Marcus, M. Palmer, L. Ramshaw, and R. Weischedel. 2006. Ontonotes: The 90% solution. In *Proceedings of NAACL-HLT*.

R. Johansson and P. Nugues. 2007. LTH: semantic structure extraction using nonprojective dependency trees. In *Proceedings of SemEval*.

T. Kleinbauer. 2012. *Generating automated meeting summaries*. Ph.D. thesis, Saarland University.

D. Liu and D. Gildea. 2010. Semantic role features for machine translation. In *Proceedings of COLING*.

L. Màrquez, X. Carreras, K. C. Litkowski, and S. Stevenson. 2008. Semantic role labeling: an introduction to the special issue. *Computational Linguistics*, 34(2):145–159.

A. Meyers, R. Reeves, C. Macleod, R. Szekely, V. Zielinska, B. Young, and R. Grishman. 2004. The NomBank project: An interim report. In *Proceedings of NAACL/HLT Workshop on Frontiers in Corpus Annotation*.

I. Meza-Ruiz and S. Riedel. 2009. Jointly identifying predicates, arguments and senses using Markov logic. In *Proceedings of NAACL-HLT*.

A. Modi, I. Titov, and A. Klementiev. 2012. Unsupervised induction of frame-semantic representations. In *Proceedings of the NAACL-HLT Workshop on the Induction of Linguistic Structure*.

M. Palmer, D. Gildea, and P. Kingsbury. 2005. The Proposition bank: An annotated corpus of semantic roles. *Computational Linguistics*, 31(1):71–106.

I. Persing and V. Ng. 2013. Modeling thesis clarity in student essays. In *Proceedings of ACL*.

J. Ruppenhofer, C. Sporleder, R. Morante, C. Baker, and M. Palmer. 2010. SemEval-2010 task 10: Linking events and their participants in discourse. In *Proceedings of SemEval*.

K. K. Schuler. 2005. *Verbnet: A Broad-coverage, Comprehensive Verb Lexicon*. Ph.D. thesis, University of Pennsylvania.

D. Shen and M. Lapata. 2007. Using semantic roles to improve question answering. In *Proceedings of EMNLP-CoNLL*.

M. Surdeanu, R. Johansson, A. Meyers, L. Màrquez, and J. Nivre. 2008. The CoNLL 2008 shared task on joint parsing of syntactic and semantic dependencies. In *Proceedings of CoNLL*.

Y. Watanabe, M. Asahara, and Y. Matsumoto. 2010. A structured model for joint learning of argument roles and predicate senses. In *Proceedings of ACL*.

B. Xie, R. J. Passonneau, L. Wu, and G. G. Creamer. 2013. Semantic frames to predict stock price movement. In *Proceedings of ACL*.

# Using Frame Semantics in Natural Language Processing

**Apoorv Agarwal**
Dept. of Computer Science
Columbia University
New York, NY
apoorv@cs.columbia.edu

**Daniel Bauer**
Dept. of Computer Science
Columbia University
New York, NY
bauer@cs.columbia.edu

**Owen Rambow**
CCLS
Columbia University
New York, NY
rambow@ccls.columbia.edu

**Abstract**

We summarize our experience using FrameNet in two rather different projects in natural language processing (NLP). We conclude that NLP can benefit from FrameNet in different ways, but we sketch some problems that need to be overcome.

## 1 Introduction

We present two projects at Columbia in which we use FrameNet. In these projects, we do not develop basic NLP tools for FrameNet, and we do not develop FramNets for new languages: we simply use FrameNet or a FrameNet parser in an NLP application. The first application concerns the extraction of social networks from narrative texts. The second application aims at generating three-dimensional pictures from textual descriptions.

The applications are very different: they differ in terms of their goals, and they differ in terms of how they use FrameNet. However, they have in common that they can use FrameNet because it provides a particular level of semantic abstraction which is suited for both applications. Consider verbs of saying, such as *declare*, *deny*, *mention*, *remark*, *tell*, or *say*: they do not have the same meaning. However, they share enough common meaning, and in particular they share the same set of participants, so that for our two applications they can be considered as interchangeable: they represent the communication of verbal information (the Message) from a Speaker to an Addressee. This is precisely what the Statement frame encodes. We will use this example in the next two sections, in which we discuss our two projects in more detail.

## 2 Using an Off-the-Shelf FrameNet Parser

Our first application is SINNET, a system that extracts a social network from narrative text. It uses the notion of a *social event* (Agarwal et al., 2010), a particular kind of event which involves (at least) two people such that at least one of them is aware of the other person. If only one person is aware of the event, we call it *Observation* (**OBS**): for example, someone is talking about someone else in their absence. If both people are aware of the event, we call it *Interaction* (**INR**): for example, one person is telling the other a story. Our claim is that links in social networks are in fact made up of social events: OBS social events give rise to one-way links, and INR social events to two-way links. For more information, see (Agarwal and Rambow, 2010; Agarwal et al., 2013a; Agarwal et al., 2013b).

From an NLP point of view, we have a difficult cluster of phenomena: we have a precise definition of what we want to find, but it is based on the cognitive state of the event participants, which is almost never described explicitly in the text. Furthermore, the definitions cover a large number of diverse situations such as talking, spying, having lunch, fist fighting, or kissing. Furthermore, some semantic differences are not relevant: verbs such as *talk*, *tell*, *deny*, all have the same meaning with respect to social events. Finally, in order to decode the events in terms of social events, we need to understand the roles: if I am talking to Sudeep about Mae, Sudeep and I have an INR social event with each other, and we both have a OBS social event with Mae. Thus, this problem sounds like an excellent application for frame semantics!

We present initial results in (Agarwal et al., 2014), and summarize them here. We use Semafor (Chen et al., 2010) as a black box to obtain the semantic parse of a sentence. However, there are several problems:

- FrameNet does not yet have complete lexical coverage.
- Semafor does not produce a single semantic



*Proceedings of Frame Semantics in NLP: A Workshop in Honor of Chuck Fillmore (1929–2014)*, pages 30–33,
Baltimore, Maryland USA, June 27, 2014. ©2014 Association for Computational Linguistics

representation for a sentence, as we would want in order to perform subsequent processing. Instead, it annotates separate, disconnected frame structures for each frame evoking element it finds.

- The data annotated with FrameNet consists of the example sentences as well as a comparatively small corpus. For this reason, it is not easy to use standard machine learning techniques for frame semantic parsing. As a result, the output is fairly errorful (as compared to, say, a state-of-the-art dependency parser trained on nearly a million annotated words). Errors include mislabeled frames, mislabeled frame elements, and missing frame elements.

To overcome these problems, we constructed several tree representations out of the partial annotations returned by Semafor. We then used tree kernels on these syntactic and semantic tree representations, as well as bags of words. The tree kernels can automatically identify important substructures in the syntactic and semantic trees without the need for feature engineering on our part. Our hypothesis is that the kernels can learn which parts of the semantic structures are reliable and can be used for prediction.

The tree structures are shown in Figure 1. The structure on the left (FrameForest) is created by taking all identified instances of frames, and collecting them under a common root node. The frame elements are filled in with dependency syntax. The structure on the right (FrameTree) is our attempt to create a single arborescent structure to capture the semantics of the whole sentence. Our third structure, FrameTreeProp (not shown), is derived from FrameTree by multiplying the nodes of interest up the path from their normal place to the root. This allows us to overcome problems with the limited locality of the tree kernels.

We present some results in Table 1. Comparing lines "Syntax" with "Synt_FrameTreeProp", we see a slight but statistically significant increase. This increase comes from using FrameNet semantics. When we look at only the semantic structures, we see that they all perform worse than syntax on its own. "BOF" is simply a bag of frames; we see that the arborescent structures outperform it, so semantic structure is useful in addition to semantic tags. "RULES" is a comprehensive set of hand-written rules we attached to frames; if frame semantic parsing were perfect, these rules should perform pretty well. They do in fact achieve the best precision of all our systems, but the recall is so low that overall they are not useful. We interpret this result as supporting our claim that part of the problem with using frame-semantic parsers is the high error rate.

| | Detection | | |
|---|---|---|---|
| Model | P | R | F1 |
| Syntax | 0.464 | 0.751 | 0.574 |
| RULES | 0.508 | 0.097 | 0.164 |
| BOF | 0.296 | 0.416 | 0.346 |
| FrameForest | 0.331 | 0.594 | 0.425 |
| FrameTree | 0.295 | 0.594 | 0.395 |
| FrameTreeProp | 0.308 | 0.554 | 0.396 |
| All | 0.494 | 0.641 | 0.558 |
| Synt_FrameTreeProp | 0.484 | 0.740 | **0.585** |

Table 1: Results for Social Event Detection. "Syntax" is an optimized model using various syntactic representations (Agarwal and Rambow, 2010). The next five models are the novel semantic features and structures. "All" refers to the model that uses all the listed structures together. "Synt_FrameTreeProp" is a linear combination of "Syntax" and FrameTreeProp.

Even though the gain so far from frame semantic parsing is small, we are encouraged by the fact that an off-the-shelf semantic parser can help at all. We are currently exploring other semantic structures we can create from the semantic parse, including structures which are dags rather than trees. We would like to point out that the combination of the parser, the creation of our semantic trees, and the training with tree kernels can be applied to any other problem that is sensitive to the meaning of text. Based on our experience, we expect to see an increase in "black box" uses of FrameNet parsing for other applications in NLP.

## 3 Extending the FrameNet Resource

FrameNet can be a useful starting point for a richer knowledge representation which is needed for a specific task. In our example, we need a representation that we can use in the WordsEye project (Coyne and Sproat, 2001), in which pictures are created automatically from text descriptions. This can be understood as providing a particular type of decompositional semantics for the input text.

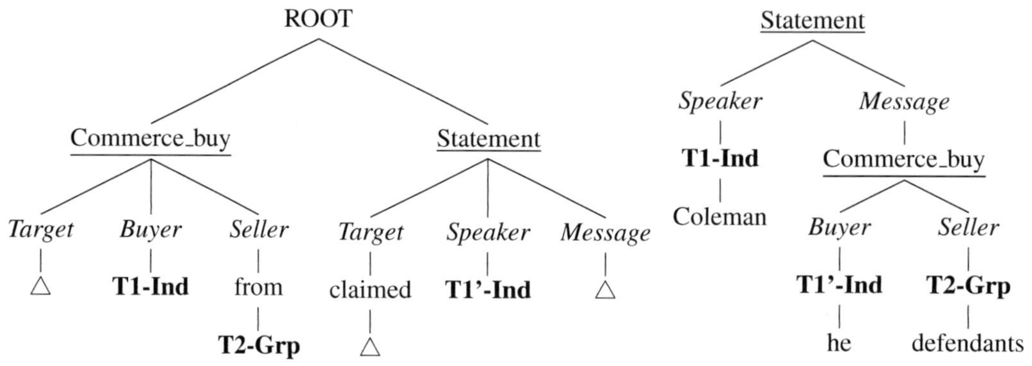


Figure 1: Semantic trees for the sentence "Coleman claimed $[\text{he}]_{T1-Ind}$ bought drugs from the $[\text{defendants}]_{T2-Grp}$.". The tree on the left is FrameForest and the tree on the right is FrameTree. △ in FrameForest refers to the subtree (bought (T1-Ind) (from T2-Grp)). **Ind** refers to individual and **Grp** refers to group.

We extend FrameNet in two ways to obtain the resource we need, which we call *VigNet* (Coyne et al., 2011).

The pictures created by the WordsEye system are based on spatial arrangements (scenes) of predefined 3D models. At a low level, scenes are described by primitive spatial relations between sets of these models (*The man is in front of the woman. He is looking at her. His mouth is open.*). We would like to use WordsEye to depict scenarios, events, and actions (*John told Mary his life story*). These can be seen as complex relations between event participants.

We turn to FrameNet frames as representations for such relations. FrameNet offers a large inventory of frames, together with additional structured information about them in the form of frame relations. Most importantly, FrameNet provides example annotations illustrating the patterns in which frames are evoked and syntactic arguments are mapped to frame elements.

However, there are two main problems if we want to turn frame annotations into pictures. First, in frame annotations frame elements are only filled with text spans, not with semantic objects. Annotations are therefore restricted to individual predicate/argument structures and do not represent the meaning of a full sentence. To address this problem we essentially use FrameNet frames as an inventory of predicates in a graph-based semantic representation. We use *semantic nodes*, which are identifiers representing events and entities that fill frame elements. Frame instances then describe relations between these semantic nodes, building a graph structure that can represent a full text fragment (including coreference). We are planning to develop parsers that convert text directly into such graph-based representations, inspired by recent work on semantic parsing (Jones et al., 2012).

Second, FrameNet frames usually describe functional relationships between frame elements, not graphical ones. To turn a frame into its graphical representation we therefore need (a) a set of of graphical frames and a formal way of decomposing these frames into primitives and (b) a mechanism for relating FrameNet frames to graphical frames. Our solution is *VigNet* (Coyne et al., 2011), an extension of FrameNet. VigNet makes use of existing frame-to-frame relations to extend FrameNet with a number of graphical frames called *Vignettes*. Vignettes are subframes of FrameNet frames, each representing a specific way in which a frame can be realized based on the specific lexical unit or on context. For instance, a proper visualization of the INGESTION frame will depend on the INGESTOR (human vs. animals of different sizes), the INGESTIBLE (different types of foods and drinks are ingested according to different social conventions, each a different Vignette). Note however, that many FrameNet frames provide useful abstractions that allow us to use a single Vignette as a good default visualization for the entire frame. For instance, all lexical units in the STATEMENT frame can be depicted as the SPEAKER standing opposite of the ADDRESSEE with an open mouth.

A new frame-to-frame relation, called *subframe parallel*, is used to decompose a Vignette into graphical sub-relations, which are in turn frames (either graphical primitives or other vignettes). Like any frame-to-frame relation, it maps frame elements of the source frame to frame elements of the target frame. New frame elements can also be introduced. For instance, one Vignette for INGESTION that can be used if the INGESTIBLE is a liquid contains a new frame element CONTAINER. The INGESTOR is holding the container and the liquid is in the container.

We have populated the *VigNet* resource using a number of different approaches (Coyne et al., 2012), including multiple choice questions on Amazon Mechanical Turk to define vignettes for locations (rooms), using the system itself to define locations, and a number of web-based annotation tools to define vignettes for actions.

An ongoing project is exploring the use of WordsEye and VigNet as a tool for field linguists and for language documentation and preservation. The WordsEye Linguistics Toolkit (WELT, (Ulinski et al., 2014)) makes it easy to produce pictures for field linguistic elicitation. It will also provide an environment to essentially develop language specific VigNets as models of the syntax/semantics interface and conceptual categories. This work may be relevant to other projects that aim to build non-English and multi-lingual FrameNets.

## 4 Conclusion

We have tried to motivate the claim that FrameNet provides the right layer of semantic abstraction for many NLP applications by summarizing two ongoing NLP projects at Columbia. We have also suggested that part of the problem in using FrameNet in NLP projects is the lack of a single structure that is produced, either in manual annotations, or in the output of a FrameNet parser. We suspect that research into how to construct such unified semantic representations will continue to be a major component of the use of FrameNet in NLP.

## Acknowledgments

This paper is based upon work supported in part by the NSF (grants IIS-0713548 and IIS-0904361), and by the DARPA DEFT Program. We thank our collaborators on the two projects used as examples in this extended abstract. We thank Chuck Fillmore for FrameNet.

## References

Apoorv Agarwal and Owen Rambow. 2010. Automatic detection and classification of social events. In *Proceedings of the 2010 Conference on Empirical Methods in Natural Language Processing*, pages 1024–1034, Cambridge, MA, October. Association for Computational Linguistics.

Apoorv Agarwal, Owen C. Rambow, and Rebecca J. Passonneau. 2010. Annotation scheme for social network extraction from text. In *Proceedings of the Fourth Linguistic Annotation Workshop*.

Apoorv Agarwal, Anup Kotalwar, and Owen Rambow. 2013a. Automatic extraction of social networks from literary text: A case study on alice in wonderland. *In the Proceedings of the 6th International Joint Conference on Natural Language Processing (IJCNLP 2013)*.

Apoorv Agarwal, Anup Kotalwar, Jiehan Zheng, and Owen Rambow. 2013b. Sinnet: Social interaction network extractor from text. In *Sixth International Joint Conference on Natural Language Processing*, page 33.

Apoorv Agarwal, Sriramkumar Balasubramanian, Anup Kotalwar, Jiehan Zheng, and Owen Rambow. 2014. Frame semantic tree kernels for social network extraction from text. In *Proceedings of the 14th Conference of the European Chapter of the Association for Computational Linguistics*, Gothenburg, Sweden.

Desai Chen, Nathan Schneider, Dipanjan Das, and Noah A. Smith. 2010. Semafor: Frame argument resolution with log-linear models. In *Proceedings of the 5th International Workshop on Semantic Evaluation*, pages 264–267, Uppsala, Sweden, July. Association for Computational Linguistics.

Bob Coyne and Richard Sproat. 2001. Wordseye: an automatic text-to-scene conversion system. In *28th annual conference on Computer graphics and interactive techniques*.

Bob Coyne, Daniel Bauer, and Owen Rambow. 2011. Vignet: Grounding language in graphics using frame semantics. In *ACL Workshop on Relational Semantics (RELMS)*, Portland, Oregon.

Bob Coyne, Alex Klapheke, Masoud Rouhizadeh, Richard Sproat, and Daniel Bauer. 2012. Annotation tools and knowledge representation for a text-to-scene system. In *COLING*, Mumbai, India.

Bevan Jones, Jacob Andreas*, Daniel Bauer*, Karl Moritz Hermann*, and Kevin Knight. 2012. Semantics-based machine translation with hyperedge replacement grammars. In *COLING*, Mumbai, India. *first authorship shared.

Morgan Ulinski, Anusha Balakrishnan, Daniel Bauer, Bob Coyne, Julia Hirschberg, and Owen Rambow. 2014. Documenting endangered languages with the wordseye linguistics tool. In *Proceedings of the ACL ComputEL workshop: The use of computational methods in the study of endangered languages*, Baltimore, MD, USA.

# Who evoked that frame? Some thoughts on context effects and event types

**Katrin Erk**
Department of Linguistics
The University of Texas at Austin
Austin, Texas 78712
katrin.erk@mail.utexas.edu

*In memoriam Charles Fillmore, 1929-2014*

**Abstract**

Lexical substitution is an annotation task in which annotators provide one-word paraphrases (lexical substitutes) for individual target words in a sentence context. Lexical substitution yields a fine-grained characterization of word meaning that can be done by non-expert annotators. We discuss results of a recent lexical substitution annotation effort, where we found strong contextual modulation effects: Many substitutes were not synonyms, hyponyms or hypernyms of the targets, but were highly specific to the situation at hand. This data provides some food for thought for frame-semantic analysis.

## 1 Introduction

Fillmore (1985) introduces the term "semantics of understanding", or U-semantics. In contrast to the semantics of truth (T-semantics), the goal of U-semantics is to "uncover the nature of the relationship between linguistic texts and the interpreter's full understanding of the texts in their contexts". A central concept of the semantics of understanding is that of the *interpretive frames* that are necessary for understanding a sentence. Frames are the "coherent schematizations of experience" underlying the words in a given sentence.

This idea of a semantics of understanding, or a frame semantics, has been made concrete in FrameNet (Fillmore et al., 2003), a large lexical database that lists frames for English words and constructions. At this point, it comprises more than 1,100 frames covering more than 12,000 lexical units (LUs), which are pairs of a term and its frame. Researchers working on other languages have adopted the FrameNet idea. Among others, there are now FrameNet resources for Spanish (Subirats and Petruck, 2003), Japanese (Ohara et al., 2004), Italian (Tonelli and Pianta, 2008; Lenci et al., 2010), as well as frame-semantic annotation for German (Erk et al., 2003).

The definition of frames proceeds in a corpus-based fashion, driven by the data (Ellsworth et al., 2004). We stand in this tradition by reporting on a recent annotation effort (Kremer et al., 2014) that collected *lexical substitutes* for content words in part of the MASC corpus (Ide et al., 2008). If we view substitute sets as indications of the relevant frame, then this data can give us interesting indicators on perceived frames in a naturally occurring text.

## 2 Lexical substitution

The Lexical Substitution task was first introduced in the context of SemEval 2007 (McCarthy and Navigli, 2009). For this dataset, annotators are asked to provide substitutes for a selected word (the *target word*) in its sentence context – at least one substitute, but possible more, and ideally a single word, though all the datasets contain some multi-word substitutes. Multiple annotators provide substitutes for each target word occurrence. Table 1 shows some examples.

By now, several lexical substitution datasets exist. Some are "lexical sample" datasets, that is, only occurrences of some selected lemmas are annotated (McCarthy and Navigli, 2009; Biemann, 2013), and some are "all-words", providing substitutes for all content words in the given sentences (Sinha and Mihalcea, 2014; Kremer et al., 2014). In addition, there is a cross-lingual lexical substitution dataset (McCarthy et al., 2013), where annotators provided Spanish substitutes for English target words in English sentence context.

Lexical substitution is a method for characterizing word meaning in context that has several attractive properties. Lexical substitution makes it possible to describe word meaning without having to rely on any particular dictionary. In addi-



*Proceedings of Frame Semantics in NLP: A Workshop in Honor of Chuck Fillmore (1929–2014)*, pages 34–37,
Baltimore, Maryland USA, June 27, 2014. ©2014 Association for Computational Linguistics

| relation | verb | noun |
|---|---|---|
| syn | 12.5 | 7.7 |
| direct-hyper | 9.3 | 7.6 |
| trans-hyper | 2.8 | 4.7 |
| direct-hypo | 11.6 | 8.0 |
| trans-hypo | 3.7 | 3.8 |
| wn-other | 60.7 | 66.5 |
| not-in-wn | 0.9 | 2.2 |

Table 2: Analysis of lexical substitution data: Relation of the substitute to the target, in percentages by part of speech (from Kremer et al. (2014))

tion, providing substitutes is a task that seems to be well doable by untrained annotators: Both Biemann (2013) and our recent annotation (Kremer et al., 2014) used crowdsourcing to collect the substitutes.[1]

## 3 Analyzing lexical substitutes

In a recent lexical substitution annotation effort (Kremer et al., 2014), we collected lexical substitution annotation for all nouns, verbs, and adjectives in a mixed news and fiction corpus, using untrained annotators via crowdsourcing. The data came from MASC, a freely available part of the American National Corpus that has already been annotated for a number of linguistic phenomena (Ide et al., 2008). All in all, more than 15,000 target tokens were annotated.

After the annotation, we performed a number of analyses in order to better understand the nature of lexical substitutes, by linking substitutes to information on WordNet (Fellbaum, 1998). Among other things, we analyzed the relation between targets and substitutes: Did substitutes tend to be synonyms, hypernyms, or hyponyms or the targets? To classify substitutes, the shortest route from any synset of the target to any synset of the substitute was used. The results are shown in Table 2, for substitutes that are synonyms (syn), hypernyms (direct-hyper, trans-hyper) and hyponyms (direct-hypo, trans-hypo) of the target. The "wn-other" line shows the percentage for substitutes that are in WordNet but not a synonym, hypo- or hypernym of the target, and "not-in-wn" are substitutes not covered by WordNet. For substitutes that are synonyms, hypernyms, and hyponyms, we see percentages between 8% and 15% for both verbs and nouns. We also see that there are few substitutes that are not in WordNet, only 1-2%. Strikingly, 60-66% of all substitutes are in WordNet, but are "wn-other": neither synonyms nor (transitive) hyponyms or hypernyms of the target. Some of these items can be viewed as missing links in the taxonomy. For example, in the second sentence of Table 2, two of the "wn-other" substitutes of *keep* are *own* and *possess*. But while *own* and *possess* are not linked to *keep* in WordNet, the FrameNet frame RETAINING, which has *keep* as a lexical unit, inherits from POSSESSION, which has both *own* and *possess* as lexical units. But this does not apply to all the "wn-other" substitutes. Some are better explained as effects of contextual modulation, fine-grained meaning distinctions that the sentence context brings about. In the first example in Table 1, there is the possibility that the speaker could be laughing at the other person, and the shoulder-clapping *clarifies* that this possibility does not correspond to the facts. In the second example in the table, the words *possess*, *enshrine* and *stage* are more specific than the substitutes that are in WordNet, and maybe more appropriate too. In the third example, the word *charge* has the meaning of *dependent*, but the situation that the sentence describes suggests that the dependents in questions may be something like *underlings* or *prisoners*.

When we look at this data from a frame-semantic analysis point of view, the first question that arises is: How specific should the frames be that are listed in FrameNet? For the second example, would we want a very specific "person as precious jewel" frame to be associated with the lexical unit "keep"? From a U-semantics point of view, one could argue that we would in fact want to have this frame, after all: It describes a recognizable abstract situation that is important for the understanding of this sentence. But it does not seem that all "wn-other" cases need to correspond to particular frames of the target word. For example, in the first sentence on Table 1, it does not seem that *clarify* should be an actual frame involving the word *show*.

From a computational linguistics point of view, a fine-grained analysis would be necessary in order to correctly predict lexical substitutes like

[1] The third example in Table 1 shows that errors do happen: The substitute "accusation" is not appropriate there. Analyses indicate that such errors are rare, though.

| sentence | substitutes |
|---|---|
| I clapped her shoulder to show I was not laughing at her. | demonstrate, express, establish, indicate, prove, convey, imply, display, *disclose*, *clarify* |
| My fear is that she would live, and I would learn that I had lost her long before Emil Malaquez translated her into a thing that can be kept, admired, and loved. | preserve, retain, hold, fix, store, *own*, *possess*, *enshrine*, *stage* |
| The distinctive whuffle of pleasure rippled through the betas on the bridge, and Rakal let loose a small growl, as if to caution his charges against false hope. | dependent, command, accusation, *private*, *companion*, *follower*, *subordinate*, *prisoner*, *teammate*, *ward*, *junior*, *underling*, *enemy*, *group*, *crew*, *squad*, *troop*, *team*, *kid* |

Table 1: Example from lexical substitution data: Target words underlined, and WordNet-unrelated substitutes shown in italics.

this – but on the other hand, experience with word sense disambiguation has shown that fine-grained senses are hard to assign with good accuracy (Palmer et al., 2007).

Another question that this data poses is: What are the items that evoke a frame? That is, what words or phrases in a sentence are responsible that a particular frame becomes important for understanding the sentence? In FrameNet it is a single lemma, multi-word expression or construction that evokes a frame. But one way of looking at the contextual modulation effects in the lexical substitution data is to say that multiple terms or constructions in the context "conspire" to make a frame relevant. In the second sentence of Table 1, we can point to multiple factors that lead to substitutes like *possess* and *enshrine*. There is fact that the THEME of *keep* is *thing*, along with the fact that the same thing is being *admired* and *loved*, and maybe also the fact that some woman had been *translated* to said thing. This thought is reminiscent of McRae and colleagues, who study general event knowledge and argue that it is not just verbs that introduce the events, but also arguments (McRae et al., 2005) and combinations of verbs and their arguments (Bicknell et al., 2010).

## References


K. Bicknell, J. Elman, M. Hare, K. McRae, and M. Kutas. 2010. Effects of event knowledge in processing verbal arguments. *Journal of Memory and Language*, 63(4):489–505.

C. Biemann. 2013. Creating a system for lexical substitutions from scratch using crowdsourcing. *Language Resources and Evaluation*, 47(1):97–122.

M. Ellsworth, K. Erk, P. Kingsbury, and S. Padó. 2004. PropBank, SALSA and FrameNet: How design determines product. In *Proceedings of the LREC Workshop on Building Lexical Resources From Semantically Annotated Corpora*, Lisbon, Portugal.

K. Erk, A. Kowalski, S. Padó, and M. Pinkal. 2003. Towards a resource for lexical semantics: A large German corpus with extensive semantic annotation. In *Proceedings of ACL*, Sapporo, Japan.

C. Fellbaum, editor. 1998. *WordNet: An electronic lexical database*. MIT Press, Cambridge, MA.

C. J. Fillmore, C. Johnson, and M. Petruck. 2003. Background to framenet. *International Journal of Lexicography*, 16(3):235–250.

C. J. Fillmore. 1985. Frames and the semantics of understanding. *Quaderni di Semantica*, 6:222–254.

N. Ide, C.F. Baker, C. Fellbaum, C. Fillmore, and R. Passonneau. 2008. MASC: The manually annotated sub-corpus of American English. In *Proceedings of LREC*, pages 2455–2461, Marrakech, Morocco.

G. Kremer, K. Erk, S. Padó, and S. Thater. 2014. What substitutes tell us - analysis of an "all-words" lexical substitution corpus. In *Proceedings of EACL*.

A. Lenci, M. Johnson, and G. Lapesa. 2010. Building an italian framenet through semi-automatic corpus analysis. In *Proceedings of LREC*, La Valletta.

D. McCarthy and R. Navigli. 2009. The English lexical substitution task. *Language Resources and Evaluation*, 43(2):139–159.

D. McCarthy, R. Sinha, and R. Mihalcea. 2013. The cross-lingual lexical substitution task. *Language Resources and Evaluation*, 47(3):607–638.

K. McRae, M. Hare, J. L. Elman, and T. Ferretti. 2005. A basis for generating expectancies for verbs from nouns. *Memory & Cognition*, 33(7):1174–1184.

K. Ohara, S. Fujii, T. Ohori, R. Suzuki, H. Saito, and S. Ishizaki. 2004. The Japanese FrameNet project: An introduction. In *Proceedings of the LREC Workshop on Building Lexical Resources from Semantically Annotated Corpora*, Lisbon, Portugal.

M. Palmer, H. Trang Dang, and C. Fellbaum. 2007. Making fine-grained and coarse-grained sense distinctions, both manually and automatically. *Natural Language Engineering*, 13:137–163.

R. Sinha and R. Mihalcea. 2014. Explorations in lexical sample and all-words lexical substitution. *Natural Language Engineering*, 20(1):99–129.

C. Subirats and M.R.L. Petruck. 2003. Surprise! Spanish FrameNet! In *Proceedings of the Workshop on Frame Semantics, XVII. International Congress of Linguists*, Prague, Czech Republic.

S. Tonelli and E. Pianta. 2008. Frame information transfer from english to italian. In *Proceedings of LREC*, Marrakech, Morocco.

# The Role of Adverbs in Sentiment Analysis

**Eduard C. Dragut**
Computer and Information Sciences Dept.
Temple University
edragut@temple.edu

**Christiane Fellbaum**
Department of Computer Science
Princeton University
fellbaum@princeton.edu

## Abstract

Sentiment Analysis, an important area of Natural Language Understanding, often relies on the assumption that lexemes carry inherent sentiment values, as reflected in specialized resources. We examine and measure the contribution that eight intensifying adverbs make to the sentiment value of sentences, as judged by human annotators. Our results show, first, that the intensifying adverbs are not themselves sentiment-laden but strengthen the sentiment conveyed by words in their contexts to different degrees. We consider the consequences for appropriate modifications of the representation of the adverbs in sentiment lexicons.

## 1 Introduction

It was probably Chuck who coined the term "armchair linguist" (Svartvik, 1991). Chuck Fillmore's deep commitment to the study of language — in particular lexical semantics — on the basis of corpus data served as a model that kept many of us honest in our investigation of language. Today, we are lucky to be able to work from our office chairs while collecting data from a broad speaker group by means of crowdsourcing. And Chuck's FrameNet taught us the importance of considering word meanings in their contexts. Our paper presents work that tries to take this legacy to heart.

## 2 Sentiment Analysis

Broadly speaking, sentiment analysis (SA) attempts to automatically derive a writer's "sentiment" about the topic of a text. "Sentiment" is usually categorized into "positive," "neutral" and "negative," where positive corresponds to satisfaction or happiness and "negative" to dissatisfaction or unhappiness. Some work in SA further distinguishes degrees of positive and negative sentiment. SA often refers to lexical resources where words are annotated with a sentiment value. SentiWordNet (SWN) (Esuli and Sebastiani, 2006) assigns one of three sentiment values to each synset in WordNet (Fellbaum, 1998). Opinion Finder (OF) (Wilson et al., 2005) identifies the sentiment of the writer. Other resources include Appraisal Lexicon (AL) (Taboada and Grieve, 2004) and Micro-WNOp (Cerini et al., 2007).

Much of this work relies on the assumption that specific lexemes (unique mappings of word forms and word meanings) carry an inherent sentiment value. This seems intuitively correct for words like *enjoy* (positive), *pencil* (neutral) and *pain* (negative).

Other words may not carry inherent sentiment value yet, in context, contribute to that of the words they co-occur with or modify. One such class of words comprises what we call *polarity intensifiers*. In this preliminary study, we analyze the contribution of *adverbial intensifiers* to the sentiment value of the sentences in which they occur.

Consider the adverb `absolutely` in two sample sentences from movie reviews:

**S1** He and Leonora have absolutely no chemistry on screen whatsoever.

**S2** I was absolutely delighted by the simple story and amazing animation.

The goal of this preliminary experimental study is to seek answers to the following questions



*Proceedings of Frame Semantics in NLP: A Workshop in Honor of Chuck Fillmore (1929–2014)*, pages 38–41,
Baltimore, Maryland USA, June 27, 2014. ©2014 Association for Computational Linguistics

| Adverbs | OF | AL | SWN |
|---|---|---|---|
| absolutely | Neu. | – | Neu. |
| awfully | Neg. | Neg. | Neu. |
| enormously | Neg. | – | Neu. |
| extremely | Neg. | – | Pos. |
| horribly | Neg. | Neg. | Neu. |
| incredibly | Pos. | Pos. | Neu. |
| pretty | Pos. | Pos. | Neu. |
| seriously | Neg. | – | Neu. |

Table 1: Eight intensifying adverbs and their polarities in sentiment lexicons.

1. Do the adverbs we investigate carry inherent sentiment values, as postulated by some sentiment lexicons?
2. Which adverbs have the strongest sentiment intensifying effect?
3. Do some adverbs have a stronger effect on sentences with a negative polarity or on sentences with a positive polarity?
4. Does the presence or absence of each adverb affect the direction of the polarity of the sentence?

## 3 The Experiment

We analyze whether human judgments show an effect on the sentiment ratings of sentences in the presence or absence of selected adverbs, and how strong the effect of each adverb is.

Let S1' be the sentence S1 from which an adverb like `absolutely` is removed. S2' is defined similarly. Three main observations can be made: (1) the adverb appears in both positive and negative sentiment-bearing sentences (S1 is negative and S2 is positive); (2) its removal from either S1 or S2 does not change the overall polarity of the sentence; (3) intuitively, S1 has a stronger negative polarity value than S1' and S2 has a stronger positive polarity value than S2'. We conduct a preliminary study of polarity intensifier words and show that they all have characteristics (1) - (3). We examine data with eight different adverbs (Table 1).

### 3.1 Data

We extracted sentences containing the target adverbs from a corpus of 50,000 movie reviews (Maas et al., 2011). Each sentence is extracted from a review that is labeled either "positive" or "negative" and correlated with a star rating. We manually inspected the sentences and discarded those where the target adverb was used in a modal sense, as in *Seriously, there was not one respectable character in the entire script* while retaining sentences like *There is no doubt that Alfred Hitchcock was a seriously talented director.* For each adverb, we retained ten sentences from positive and negative reviews each, for a total 160 sentences. We copied the original sentences, removed the adverbs without making additional alterations. Our final dataset consisted of a total of 320 sentences with 160 sentence pairs whose members were identical except for the presence or absence of the target adverbs. Below is an example of a sentence pair, where the original sentence with the adverbs was pre-classified by (Pang and Lee, 2004) as carrying positive sentiment.

1. I was <u>absolutely</u> delighted by the simple story and amazing animation.
2. I was delighted by the simple story and amazing animation.

### 3.2 Collecting Judgments via Crowdsourcing

We submitted single sentences (not pairs) to be annotated with sentiment scores for crowdsourcing, using Amazon Mechanical Turk (AMT). To avoid any bias we shuffled the sentences and displayed them individually. We asked the Turkers to select, for each sentence, one of five sentiment scores: strong positive (2), positive (1), neutral (0), negative (-1), strong negative (-2). Each sentence was rated by five annotators. Altogether, twenty annotators completed the task within eight hours. Since the annotators did not all judge the same set of sentences, we computed the agreement between annotators as follows. For each annotator, his/her agreement with the others is given be the following formula: $\frac{1}{|S(i)|}\sum_{j\in S(i)} ps_{ji}$,

where $S(i)$ is the set of sentences annotated by the i$^{th}$ Turker and $ps_{ji}$ is the percentage of Turkers who have the same annotation with the i$^{th}$ Turker for sentence $j$. $|S(i)|$ is the cardinality of set $S(i)$. The agreement ranges from 0.52 to 0.8. Although the annotation of some Turkers is close to that of flipping a coin, all judgments were retained and included in the results reported here.

### 3.3 Results

We report the main results. The polarity rating of a sentence $j$ is the (un-weighted) average rating

| Adverbs | Avg. Pol. Change | Pol. Reversal |
|---|---|---|
| absolutely | 0.2 | 0/20 |
| awfully | **0.6** | 2/20 |
| enormously | 0.2 | 1/20 |
| extremely | 0.2 | 2/20 |
| horribly | 0.2 | 0/20 |
| incredibly | 0.2 | 4/20 |
| pretty | 0.2 | 1/20 |
| seriously | **0.4** | 3/20 |

Table 2: Effects of adverbs on sentiment ratings.

of the five annotators for the sentence, denoted $\alpha_j$ and $\alpha_j = \sum_i ps_{ji}$. We use uniform weighting. A sentence $j$ is classified into one of the five polarity categories according to the following criteria:

| | |
|---|---|
| strong positve | if $\alpha_j \in [1.5, 2]$ |
| positive | if $\alpha_j \in (1.5, 0.5]$ |
| neutral | if $\alpha_j \in (0.5, -0.5)$ |
| negative | if $\alpha_j \in [-0.5, -1.5)$ |
| strong negative | if $\alpha_j \in [-0.5, -2]$ |

#### 3.3.1 Do Adverbs Change Sentiment Rating?

We first examine the polarity intensifying effects of the eight adverbs and determine their relative intensifying effects. For each adverb we compute the average polarity rating change between the members of the 20 sentence pairs with and without the target adverb. The second column of Table 2 shows the average polarity rating change for the adverbs. All adverbs have polarity intensifying effect, which ranges from 0.2 to 0.6. `Awfully` and `seriously` have the strongest effect.

#### 3.3.2 Change of Sentiment Rating in Positive vs. Negative Contexts

Next we ask whether the adverbs have a stronger polarity intensifying effect on sentences with a negative, positive or neutral ratings. We partition the 20 sentences with/without each adverb into the three polarity categories according to their average polarity ratings. A sentence $j$ is negative (positive) if $\alpha_j \leq -0.5$ ($\alpha_j \geq 0.5$). Figure 1 shows the results. For six out of the eight adverbs, the graph follows a V-shaped pattern, indicating that the adverbs have stronger polarity influence on sentences conveying opinionated, but not neutral, statements. `Pretty` shows the weakest effect across, which makes intuitive sense, as this adverb seems to have a "softening/weakening" effect: consider "pretty good," which one could judge to be slightly less good than "good." For example, the sentence

*He has a pretty strident rant about how important it is.*

received an average rating score of 0 with the adverb present and -0.2 without it. The results for `awfully` and `extremely` are surprising. A closer look at the annotations revealed some possible unreliable ratings. For example, the sentence

*The part of the movie set in Vietnam was extremely inaccurate.*

has average polarity score of 0 (i.e., neutral) with the adverb and -0.8 without. Intuitively, it seems that the first sentence conveys a strong negative sentiment. Such data indicate the need for further study. A more complex scheme for computing the average polarity scores, such as weighted by inter-annotator agreement, might produce better results.

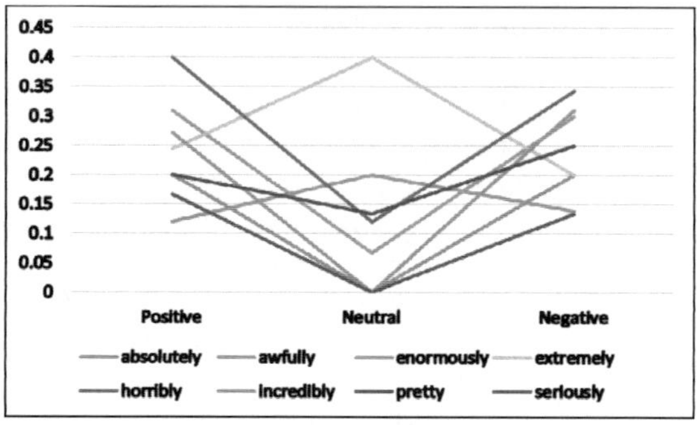


Figure 1: The polarity intensifying effects of adverbs over the sentiment categories.

#### 3.3.3 Can Adverbs Reverse Sentiment Orientation?

We ask whether their presence can have the effect of reversing the polarity of a sentence. We again consider three sentiment categories: positive, negative and neutral. The third column in Table 2 shows for each adverb, how many sentences out of the total of 20 were judged to have a reversed polarity when the adverb was removed. Overall, the polarities of only 13 out of 160 sentences (i.e., about 8%) change.

#### 3.3.4 Do Adverbs Have an Inherent Sentiment Value?

Our target adverbs have inherent polarity as claimed in some sentiment lexicons (see Table 1).

If the polarity of a sentence does not change when the adverbs is present or absent, we conclude that the adverb has no inherent polarity but may merely affect the intensity of the constituents that it modifies. These results, as displayed in Figure 1 indicate that our target adverbs do not carry inherent polarity. Instead, they modify the intensity of the sentiment connoted by the context.

## 4 Discussion

We examined the effect of eight intensifying adverbs on the sentiment ratings of the sentences in which they occur. Our study showed that, contrary to their representation in some widely used sentiment lexicons, these adverbs do not carry an inherent sentiment polarity, but merely alter the degree of the polarity of the constituents they modify; corrections of the corresponding entries in the sentiment resources seem warranted. Our results show further that all adverbs strengthen the polarity of the context to different degrees. If confirmed on a larger data set, this indicates that the intensifying force of different adverbs should be reflected in lexical resources, perhaps along an ordered scale.

## 5 Related Work

Two recent surveys give a detailed account of the SL acquisition techniques (Feldman, 2013; Liu, 2012). We give only an overview of the related work here. SLs are acquired by one of three methods. Manual tagging is performed by human annotators: e.g., OF, and AL. Dictionary-based acquisition relies on a set of seed words that is expanded by using external resources, such as WordNet: e.g., (Dragut et al., 2010; Hassan and Radev, 2010; Mohammad et al., 2009; Dragut et al., 2012; Takamura et al., 2005). In corpus-based acquisition a set of seed words is expanded by using a large corpus of documents (Feng et al., 2013; Lu et al., 2011; Yu et al., 2013; Wu and Wen, 2010).

To our knowledge, none of these works include the polarity intensifiers that we introduce in this paper.

## References


S. Cerini, V. Compagnoni, A. Demontis, M. Formentelli, and G. Gandini, 2007. *Language resources and linguistic theory: Typology, second language acquisition, English linguistics.*

Eduard C. Dragut, Clement T. Yu, A. Prasad Sistla, and Weiyi Meng. 2010. Construction of a sentimental word dictionary. In *CIKM*, pages 1761–1764.

Eduard C. Dragut, Hong Wang, Clement Yu, Prasad Sistla, and Weiyi Meng. 2012. Polarity consistency checking for sentiment dictionaries. In *ACL*.

A. Esuli and F. Sebastiani. 2006. Sentiwordnet: A publicly available lexical resource for opinion mining. In *LREC*.

Ronen Feldman. 2013. Techniques and applications for sentiment analysis. *CACM*, 56(4):82–89, April.

C. Fellbaum. 1998. *WordNet: An On-Line Lexical Database and Some of its Applications.* MIT Press.

Song Feng, Jun Sak Kang, Polina Kuznetsova, and Yejin Choi. 2013. Connotation lexicon: A dash of sentiment beneath the surface meaning. In *ACL*.

Ahmed Hassan and Dragomir Radev. 2010. Identifying text polarity using random walks. In *ACL*.

Bing Liu. 2012. *Sentiment Analysis and Opinion Mining*. Synthesis Lectures on Human Language Technologies. Morgan & Claypool Publishers.

Yue Lu, Malu Castellanos, Umeshwar Dayal, and ChengXiang Zhai. 2011. Automatic construction of a context-aware sentiment lexicon: an optimization approach. In *WWW*, pages 347–356. ACM.

Andrew L. Maas, Raymond E. Daly, Peter T. Pham, Dan Huang, Andrew Y. Ng, and Christopher Potts. 2011. Learning word vectors for sentiment analysis. In *ACL*, pages 142–150.

Saif Mohammad, Cody Dunne, and Bonnie Dorr. 2009. Generating high-coverage semantic orientation lexicons from overtly marked words and a thesaurus. In *EMNLP*.

B. Pang and L. Lee. 2004. A sentimental education: Sentiment analysis using subjectivity summarization based on minimum cuts. In *ACL*.

Jan Svartvik, editor. 1991. *Directions in Corpus Linguistics*. Nobel Symposium 82, Mouton de Gruyter.

M. Taboada and J. Grieve. 2004. Analyzing appraisal automatically. In *AAAI Spring Symposium*.

Hiroya Takamura, Takashi Inui, and Manabu Okumura. 2005. Extracting semantic orientations of words using spin model. In *ACL*, pages 133–140.

T. Wilson, J. Wiebe, and P. Hoffmann. 2005. Recognizing contextual polarity in phrase-level sentiment analysis. In *HLT/EMNLP*.

Yunfang Wu and Miaomiao Wen. 2010. Disambiguating dynamic sentiment ambiguous adjectives. In *COLING*, pages 1191–1199.

Hongliang Yu, Zhi-Hong Deng, and Shiyingxue Li. 2013. Identifying sentiment words using an optimization-based model without seedwords. In *ACL*.

# Author Index